3-

MW01148264

To Jamie and Kristy,

Thanks very much for supporting my first book and coming to my open studio — more books on the way —

Warm Regards

Sandy

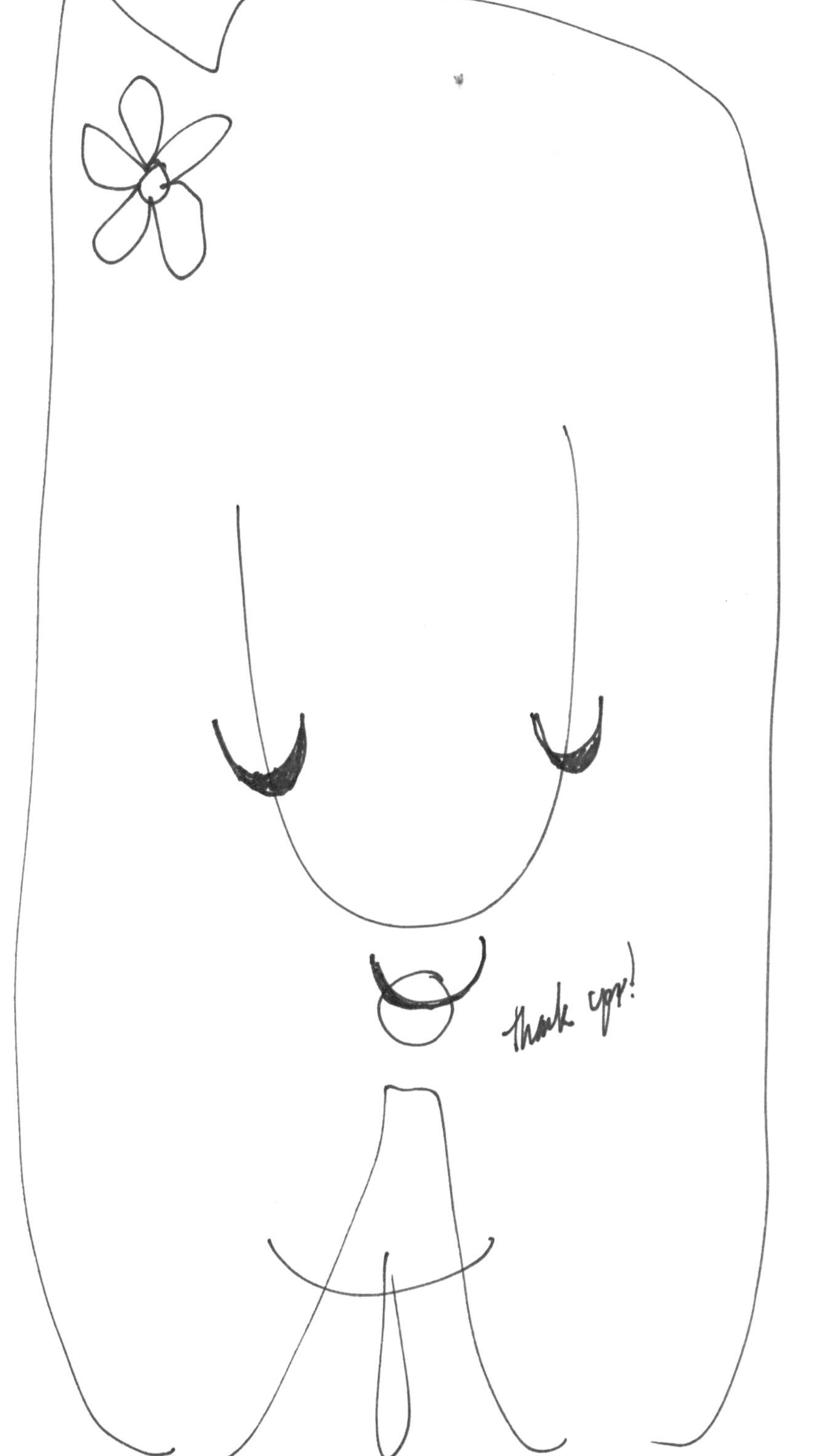
thank you!

The original handwritten journal of *Baloney*

"It doesn't matter that you lost the file with your first draft and it doesn't matter how long this has been on the shelf. Go back to the old journal, start a new file, edit the document, make a book and get it out there. You need to publish this story."

- Deborah Shea, Senior Independent Advisor
for the first draft of Baloney Express
College Writing Professor, St. Lawrence University

"An honest coming of age story, unlike some famous recovery books that are fictional and therefore disrespectful to their readers. I strongly recommend a slice of Baloney."

- H.T., Anonymous Patient in Recovery

"I loved Baloney Express. I read it in two days. The author completely understands what it feels like to be in here. I will read it again, a journal entry a day, as I go through my recovery. I will refer to this book now and in the future. Everyone at the clinic wants to read it. We need more copies."

- B.D., Anonymous Patient in Recovery

"Earnest and amusing. A quick, insightful, enjoyable read. A three train ride book. Let me put it this way... that other whiny memoir I started long before I picked up Baloney two days ago sits in my trunk unread, where it will probably live all winter."

- Christopher Peter, Astute Cultural Critic

"It is a real experience to read with the author as he grows intellectually and spiritually through Baloney Express. At times very funny, at times poignant, this strong and honest coming of age story will reach people. An impressive debut book that should be passed down the line."

- K. Young, Online Book Reviews

Other Published Works

Art:

Sandy Garnett Paintings & Sculptures Inventory
(Annual Editions)
ISBN - 978-0-9822348-4-6

More art books coming in 2011

Children:

The Rainbow Riders
ISBN - 978-0-9822348-1-5

The Rainbow Riders ABC Book
ISBN - 978-0-9822348-2-2

More Rainbow Riders books coming soon

www.rainbowriderskids.com

Music:

Sandy Garnett's songs are available
at online music retailers

www.baloneyexpress.com

All of the above can be found at

www.sandygarnett.com

BALONEY EXPRESS

A DEBUT BOOK BY

SANDY GARNETT

Chelsea Press

Printed in the United States of America.

ISBN 978-0-9822348-3-9 - hardcover

Baloney Express

Published by

Chelsea Press

A Division of Chelsea Multimedia
Graphics 2000 Inc.

For bulk orders and correspondence:

inquiries@chelseapress.com

www.sandygarnett.com

Cover Painting by Sandy Garnett,
'Mesa Walk', oil on canvas, 20 x 14 inches, 2010.

All images within book were done by Sandy Garnett

with the exception of Auguste Rodin's 'Le Penseur', 1880.

For Ted

&

My Family

This story is taken
from the author's journal entries.

Names used in this book
have been changed.

Contents

© Sandy Garnett, *Maze*, ink on paper, 14 x 11 inches, high school senior year.

BALONEY EXPRESS

High school senior spring

1

The Setup

Freshman Year Winter

© Sandy Garnett, *Self-Portrait In Shattered Mirror*, college freshman fall.

24 January

I have dissolved into a sea of wicked hangovers, blank evenings, forgotten social events, scrapes with authority, the drinking carving every dimension of my freshman year as I wallow in this pit of depression and despair. Drunken blackouts have damaged my mind and body. I cannot continue on this path of self-destruction I have put my drunk self into. My life can and will change... it must change.

How is it to be a party guy who means well but whose weakened will has fallen into a dark pattern of instant gratification? It's not a fun job. The endeavor requires strength, endurance, routine and stupidity.

Now I am drinking daily with the intent of oblivion. Half a bottle of liquor, a case of beer, drugs to keep me drinking. Wasted is powerful and numbingly pleasing. The alcohol and drugs wash my worries away every time I go to them, but they only ease the pain temporarily.

I finally come to my senses and shut off the alarm clock, which has been ringing for an hour. Shit. I missed my class again. Second time this week and it's only Wednesday. My lights are on and the door is ajar. What happened last night?

God I was wasted. Let's see, I remember until about 9pm or so when we left Joe's room for that party. What do I have to do today? My head is absolutely swimming as I stagger to my knees and scratch my aching back. My boxers are ripped and my jacket doesn't appear to be in my room. I always forget my jackets. Where did I leave that damn thing anyway? I have a large bruise on my thigh and my finger sports a nasty cigarette burn. My hands are peppered with scars from the burning cherries of cigarettes that crater my fingers in wasted stupors. I feel numbness in both of my arms up to my elbows as I saunter to the bathroom and urinate, looking in the mirror at a 19-year-old who spends a minute a day studying his exhausted and saddened young face, crushed by another late night blackout.

I want a cigarette but can't find the reserve that I always keep under my chair for these painful waking moments every single morning. What was her name again? She seemed pretty cute. I want a girlfriend. The drunk leaves me lonely and yearning for someone to love as I cannot love, but rather hate myself. A bong hit might be nice right now. The daily wake and bake puts me out of my misery and keeps me high for part of the day. I smoke what is left of a joint from the tin. I need more.

I walk downstairs into a friend's room. I wake him up and ask him what we did last night, where he saw me last as we'd gone out together. He coughs, swears, and has no idea what I did last night, although we likely spent most of the evening within eyeshot of each other at the same party. Another friend saunters in to join us, whipping off a story about his luck with a nice girl he brought home. He tells me he last saw me passed out on the couch at Jon's. I tell him that I found myself in my room this morning, so I got home okay. The passing out thing gets me in trouble. Some mornings I find myself at the foot of my dorm room door in the hallway because I couldn't punch in the combo, in an unfamiliar dorm room or lounge, outside if there is no ice. This is dangerous because school is cold and the region loses a local a year who passes out in the bush, is snowed over and found in the spring thaw. I never remember going to bed. We joke some more and discuss plans, where to get more weed and what's going on tonight. We eat dinner and get booze for the early evening. I shower, dress, clean my room to conceal the emptiness of my disheveled, miserable lifestyle, then I start drinking shots again on the way to another blackout.

This is how I have spent my freshman year at college. Partying has taken me over. All of the problems I've had in the past several years are directly linked to my absurd drinking habits. Once I have a drink, I feel this unleashed desire to consume fast and hard until I reach that state of oblivion again. I look three or four drinks ahead of the one I have in my hand. I am never satisfied with the buzz until memory fades and I no longer have to focus on drinking so much to forget.

It is a riot to be a party guy, but there is too much drunkenness, too many problems at school, in trouble, with concerned friends asking about me, so I minimize my blackouts with most people. Lately I've got friends who have been looking to cut me off if I get too wasted, so I have to keep my buzz under wraps more. Many of my friends party hard as well, so I conceal my extreme party habits with my hard party friends. This is troubling.

I spend all of my time now feeding this fire as weeks fade into months. My spirit feels hollow, frayed, drawn.

I have to make a change soon before I do damage that cannot be undone.

Written 4 months before Day 1

Freshman Year of College
(during a one week suspension as a result of drinking)

2

The Rehab

© Sandy Garnett, *Maze*, ink on paper, freshman year spring.

Day 1 Sunday, May 21

I was woken at 7am by the puffy charge nurse with bouncy red curls that offset her tremendous thighs, I showered in a jail-like cubicle and proceeded to the detox station, where my bodily vitals were taken again by a pretty blonde piping bitch on this most miserable Sunday of my life.

Yesterday was admittance day. My parents drove me up, my mother sledding in stony silence that iced over the car and my heart, my father highlighting the positives. I am not far from home but a world away.

A check-in clerk asked me admittance questions. What is my drug of choice... when was my last drug use... do I have any ill effects from not having used my drug of choice today... has my drug usage created trauma in my world, has it created trouble for me, to what degree... is my memory intact... am I violent on or off said drug of choice... have I killed people as a result of my drug abuse... do I have trouble sleeping when not on said drug of choice... am I a stupid idiot for getting a second DWI four days ago that landed me here in rehab with my dunce cap on, answering cursory drug behavior questions with this administrative gatekeeper and so on. I was told that our discussion would be kept completely confidential, although this guy was scribbling furiously, he would talk about me at lunch with his colleagues and my file will exist in handwritten record for eternity unless the place burns down.

During our 'family discussion' a preliminary interviewer sprang the concept of an adolescent program on me. It was only when he mentioned that the adolescent program was seven weeks long that I began to defend myself against that long of a stay. I had been informed that my rehabilitation would last four weeks and no longer, so I started to argue with the guy. Dad immediately sided with me, thankfully, but Mom agreed with the 'professional'. I was sent away to an adjacent table where I sat impatiently. The interviewer took note of my behavior, pencil to chin, searching for just the right words to jot down, waiting for me to combust. When I was waved back to the conversation I was completely relieved to hear that I would be joining the adult program, although I showed no satisfaction.

After a bland, gray, awkward lunch my parents slipped away and I was left to speak more about my drug and drinking history. I am not familiar with all of the ridiculous rehab language but I'm starting to pick up on it. After another physical I was led to a temporary room where my belongings were dumped on the bed and sifted through for drugs. I am here for drinking but it's all the same to these people. Nurse Ratched found no smack in my belongings. I am surprised she didn't bend me over in search of a spare eight ball. The nurse did take my hacky sack (maybe I should have shoved that up there), a water bottle, a Grateful Dead tee shirt and half of my toiletries. Standard procedure she explained, sloshing around my confiscated mouthwash. Then I was cattled to another room referred to as the detox lounge. After receiving a pile of reading material and forms I began to fill out some of this crap.

At 3:30pm I was led down to my first AA meeting. I took a seat and listened to a tall balding glass of water with darting mouse eyes at the dais nervously detail the tragic pitfalls and perils of his drug addiction. When he finished there was a standing ovation and the emotional speaker stooped back to his seat, embraced by people on the way. This odd procession came as a shock, but later in the evening I realized that this is standard procedure in the lives of recovering boozers and junkies. The meeting closed with everyone holding hands and reciting an unfamiliar prayer. The last token words shouted in unison were fittingly, "It works if you work it so work it, it's worth it." Dr. Seuss on crack.

After detox lounge time and a drab dinner I was bombarded by another AA-like meeting that lasted for an hour. People are talking about weird, sensitive shit that I don't want to hear. I guess I have to get used to it though. I'll have to sweat it out for a month in this place.

I got to sleep at midnight and woke up early this morning. I showered and made my way to the nurse's camp; the pulse, the blood pressure, the temperature, the coy conversation. After breakfast the same nurse repeated my vitals. What, do they think I'll kick the bucket on them? I'm a young buck of nineteen. I bet some of the old farts are wheeled in on their deathbeds so the rehab has to cover its bureaucratic ass. I guess hooked people can have nasty withdrawals... some lose bowel control, tear their eyes out, commit suicide, attack the charges, hallucinate, some have seizures, heart attacks, these sorts of things. I've seen people do all of this while driving an ambulance in high school as an EMT and at Grateful Dead concerts, creetching amidst the twirling hall dancers, naked in the stairwells, minds popping while the humanity drains away, the horror stricken faces, the whites of eyes peering out of the darkness.

Before lunch a shrink gave me a memory test. I was shown a series of graphic designs marked by numbers on cue cards. When the tester took them away I had to draw the proper design according to the number she shot at me. I found a piece of gum on the underside of the table and wondered if this person had been admitted for crack or heroin, if she was pretty, what she had been wearing, how she had done at this game. I scored nine out of ten. Pigtails told me that three out of ten is exceptional and I laughed with her for a hearty moment. There have to be some twisted souls checking into this place. I'm here anyway.

I was shuffled in to see another administrator, whose job consists of form filling and giving patients the 'treatment plan' pitch. We spoke about my problem and I sat enthralled while the stocky pink gentleman explained how this treatment would help me. He concluded by telling me not to worry, that I'd be all right. I thanked him graciously for his words of wisdom, as though I need anyone to tell me how I'll be in this fucking shithole. I filled out some more standard forms then went to lunch.

Back at the nurse's station, I enjoyed a pleasant chat with one of the physician's assistants about my college. At least those in positions of authority are treating me with some respect, although they are most likely paid to sound interested.

I just got back from a lengthy AA 'speaker meeting', which was like the one yesterday. I am sitting in the detox lounge, merrily detoxing. My white bracelet will soon be replaced by a green bracelet and I will graduate into the broader 'community', this mysterious place beyond those big blue doors at the end of the vacuous detoxification wing. I love the bracelet concept. What a novelty.

Day 2 Monday, May 22

Last night I joined the 'community', and after the Narcotics Anonymous meeting I moved my stuff into room B2. My new roommate is Don. He seems nice enough, a middle-aged junkie with bad hair, a pot belly and severe stutter, mostly a quiet, brooding guy. We are all brooding here, everyone has that faraway gaze, remembering the good and the bad, the buzz we all miss and came here to expunge from our tormented souls. Don's old roommate Dick moved out yesterday. The night before last the community made concentric rocking circles around him while singing his requested 'Amazing Grace'. He fell weepy into their arms. Yuck. Apparently Dick's a dick so people were glad to see him leave. After all the hoopla celebrating his long awaited departure he walked back in the door today with his tail between his legs because his halfway house had made a clerical error. Six hours of driving for nothing, his old room is now filled by me so he waits in purgatory temp space with a couple of wet brains in pampers until Thursday. Shit luck Dick.

There are three male wings and two female wings, fifteen to a wing, two to a room and each wing has a smallish lounge. The interior is decorless, the furniture cheap and institutional yet sturdy for good cries, the colors neutral, the carpets patterned gray to hide the dirt. Each wing does a 7:30am meditation. We read the thought for the day in a little book called "24 Hours a Day Book" and have a short discussion about the passage. This morning we talked about serenity and I got a feel for this daily ritual.

After meditation we first-weekers went to the dining room, where a number of exciting red tape forms and analytical tests eagerly awaited our arrival. The last and most extensive test was a 550 question survey that measures intelligence, psychology, motivations. I kicked ass on the thing and was the first one out of ten to finish, but those hard core questions were sufficient to catnap me after lunch until the next meeting. Funny... I was first one out of the test yay! I've got that old competitive edge in REHAB!

A couple cups of coffee later I went to my first group therapy session. Group therapy is from 1:30 to 3pm every day except for Sundays. I was one of two newcomers today. I have been hanging out with a guy named Pat, who was admitted the same day I was. Pat is a forty-something captain in charge of one of the jail setups in Manhattan. He is medium height and build, he's got brown hair, dark eyebrows, a moustache, a friendly face, and he wears black, square-rimmed glasses. He seems like a decent guy who has seen a lot. He introduced himself to the group and explained that he admitted himself for drinking and cocaine, detailing some of his habits. I followed by introducing myself to the group. For the first time since I walked in these doors I began to wonder if I might really have a substance abuse problem as I sat in a ring of druggies and told pieces of my story.

During my brief introduction to the group I began to rationalize and leave out some of the things I had gotten into. From what the counselor explained, an alcoholic is as good as a drug addict, whether drugs are his problem or not. I'm beginning to realize the sense in this, but for some reason I am rejecting the label of addict as well as alcoholic. Drugs aren't my problem as I've only been smoking weed daily for a year, so why should I call myself an addict?

I left therapy group frustrated and came back to my new residence to draw. This is one of my favorite things to do, a nice outlet, stress reliever, always has been since I could hold a crayon. I began to rationalize again as the pencil moved around the paper. I have a problem because I was hit with two DWI's, so my problem is that I'm unlucky. I was not out of control at college last spring semester. Why do I hang on proudly to the fact that with heavy self-monitoring I blacked out less than I did freshman fall? What led to my self-monitoring? I was suspended for a week as a result of my drinking so I was trying to keep a lid on it all spring, which I kind of did. Does this constitute control? I returned for summer break a week ago and the night of my first DWI class, which had been postponed for me to attend my first year of college, I walked out of class pissed, I got blotto and nailed for a second DWI several hours later. This reads like a trashy novel, my trashy novel. Why do I deny that I have a problem? I'm afraid, confused and I have so many stinging questions about my present state.

As I draw I formulate my argument with which to debate the entire community. I matured so much at school but forgot to bring my newfound wisdom home with me the day I returned. Not bad but I don't know if I can sell it.

Tina paged me for my first case manager interview. I told her that I'm not sure whether or not I'm an alcoholic, putting into play the newly rationalized 'maturity left at college' argument. So far I've impressed the staff with my snappy responses and decent insight, but my defensive humor and wit do not solve any problems, according to my case manager. For the first time since I was admitted I saw a back door and ran through it, language used to pin down the fleeting rationale of addicts. Rationalizing a problem is fighting the problem, which creates a weakness in the individual who seeks recovery. Tina suggested these things patiently, sapping me slowly over the course of our meeting. The more one fights the weaker one becomes. This is what I have been doing, fighting, resisting, and by the third afternoon meeting I was feeling exposed and depleted.

Discussion group was interesting and helped me come to my senses. This is one of the few meetings I am allowed to choose for myself. Most people here qualify themselves as crack or cocaine addicts, heroin users or pill poppers, so there are specific groups for these people. Meetings line my day and variations like this one splinter into strange categories like a one hour group discussion on the subject of 'coping'. The coping meeting applied more broadly to my drunken ass than the other drug specific meetings so I chose this one.

Al's coping group was filled with old, beat up drunks who are hooked on the heavy drugs. I was the youngest by fifteen years. Most of the younger patients are cocaine or crack addicts. Talking with older people doesn't make me uncomfortable, even though they have children my age. The adult group is where I belong. The adolescent program is heavily monitored, they march around like chain gangs, their cigarettes are allotted, lights out 9pm. "Give us all your clothing and cigarettes. You won't be needing these gang colors while you enjoy your seven week vacation with us." Screw that shit. The adolescents walk around in hospital gowns with scowls, which wouldn't help me much. My bad attitude is so much more mature. There are ten or fifteen people my age or older in the adult group of ninety residents. Whatever the age or problem, everyone here is treated equally, which is a comfort to my blistered ego.

Al started his meeting. I introduced myself and gave a brief history, employing my new 'maturity left at college' concept. Maybe Tina listened to my angle but suddenly I'm sitting in a lion's den of bullshit masters who have been lying to themselves longer than I've been alive. I battled off their pointed suggestions that I was fooling myself. They were all thinking that I'm new and I'll get it one of these days, which pissed me off because they were right. Fighting had weakened me. At the end of the meeting I reprimanded myself for my defensive behavior and the group thanked me for my honesty. I felt better for the admission but I felt stupid for getting picked off for trying to skate around the truth. Why do I hang on proudly to the fact that with a lot of self-monitoring I managed not to black out or pass out quite as much in the past four months? That doesn't necessarily constitute control now, does it? And I got pinched for a second DWI the day I got home from my freshman year at college, which is pathetic. Why do I continue to deny the fact that I've been a blackout drunk for the past year?

After dinner we all went to the first week lecture and listened to Mel, a respected therapist, as he explained the first step of recovery. There is a guide referred to as the 'Steps of Recovery', which outlines the twelve emotional steps that any recovering individual should follow in order to stay sober and find that intangible thing called serenity, something everyone gallops after around here. The first step is said to be the largest obstacle in the recovery of an alcoholic or addict:

Step 1

"We admitted that we were powerless over alcohol (or drugs) and that our lives had become unmanageable."
- Alcoholics Anonymous

The first step is the beginning of a long road, which I am told is a life process with no end. Mel was a good speaker and I learned some interesting things, although my mind was elsewhere during the lecture. I kept daydreaming about where I would be watching the sunset if I were home... a barbecue with best friends at a beach house on the water, a party, pretty girls, the perfect summer evening. But here I was, reality grinding me down, surrounded by a bunch of fuck-ups talking about this 'step' program, freaking out, crying, swearing, bitching. Why me? Denial. Denial is something I am starting to recognize intellectually. This is no fun. It hurts, it sucks, it saddens and is the last thing I want to do in the virgin days of summer. Who's bitching now?

After the meeting I walked out to the lounge and bumped into Josh, another young guy I've laughed with a couple of times who is in my group. We talked about my mention of LSD in therapy, that my numerous experiences went far beyond the experimentation I admitted to in group. I explained my confusion about whether or not I have a problem. We lit smokes and checked out the moon on the smoker's deck. Josh said that it was good for him to let it all out here. I understood and appreciated his passive support. This is his third trip to rehab and the kid is younger than me... booze, pot, pills, coke, whatever he can get his hands on.

I can't get away from my age and position in life right now. I'm too young to get sober! I just finished my freshman year and right when things were looking up I got pinched for another DWI. I have three years left of college before I get serious with this recovery shit! The last thing I need is rehab. How the hell can I go back to college and not have a beer or a smoke, tell me that! Fuck, fuck, fuck.

On a reassuring note, Josh told me something that may be very important if I'm ever going to take this seriously. He told me that when he was sober last year for four months he stayed clean day by day. By putting off the party day by day and chipping away at time, he didn't have to face the dismal aspect of never being able to get wasted again. He told me that the farther he got in recovery, the easier sobriety became. It seems true but hard as hell and I don't want to do that. Well, as they say in rehab, "Tomorrow is another day."

Day 3 Tuesday, May 23

In the morning I had my first-week lecture. The counselor talked about how each family member assumes a role to complete the family unit. This subconscious system of role playing and reinforcement can lead to what she called 'a dysfunctional family'. There is the hero, the scapegoat, and the mascot. More often than not the roles played by siblings in the family occur respectively, according to age. The oldest is often the hero, the middle sibling(s) the scapegoat(s), and the youngest the mascot. She also suggested that there were various pressures placed upon and felt by each role player. The hero is expected to perform, the scapegoat becomes complacent and accepts much of the family burden, and the mascot lives in a sheltered and carefree manner, making ultimate independence and emotional stability difficult. The lecture was good and it stimulated me to analyze my family situation a bit. My youngest brother Christian has always been the mascot as he is much younger, but my younger brother Matthew and I have traded the hero and scapegoat roles at various times in our lives. Matt has been the hero for several years now and I have been the tormented scapegoat.

My next meeting was my first fitness class. Randy was my partner and we spent the class doing a 'trust' exercise where one person leads his blindfolded partner around a given area nonverbally. Each of us had to go for about five minutes. Randy and I were laughing about the whole thing from start to finish.

Randy is a jacked-up weight lifter and wrestler, five foot ten inches tall and workout wide, with a buzz cut afro, a mustache, and piercing eyes that contain humor at every turn. He used to be a counselor for troubled teens but gave it up for wrestling. He routinely gets beaten up by the Hulk Hogans of the game. He says that with a lot of work he can get a name for himself in professional wrestling. It looks like he knows about performance enhancing supplements but I'll never ask. Randy was into heroin for awhile, hanging out in shooting galleries. Shooting galleries are abandoned tenements where junkies shoot dope. He said that these places are disgusting, filled with blood, vomit, urine and feces, poverty, insanity, theft, rape, overdose, death, murder. One time, when he was shooting dope, one of his fellow addicts died right there in front of Randy and his doping friends. I asked what his friends in the room did. "They tossed him out of the third story window into an alley and split up his dope," Randy casually mentioned with a self-reflecting chuckle.

Everyone here has crazy stories, then they get sober and are all nice nice. Go figure. That story doesn't do justice to Randy now, not sober anyway. He's one of the funniest people I've ever met, and we have spent most of our free time in the lounge laughing our asses off, making sport of cracking each other up. If I have a best friend in this place now it's Randy.

Shortly after fitness class I was paged to interview with one of the staff psychologists. It seems like my interviewers have been mildly impressed by my conversations with them. Maybe this is my inflated ego talking as I'm just another boozer who got in big trouble, which is not very impressive. There is no way around it so I might as well not lie to myself or hide that anymore.

Young Adult Group followed lunch. The typical rehab patient goes through about seven hours of therapy, meetings and group discussions a day. This sucks but I am getting used to it. In our discussion we talked about the activities to be involved with and the activities to stay away from in the real world, once we get out of here. We discussed the 'little voice' inside all of our fucked up heads that instinctively lead us back to our 'drugs of choice' and how difficult it becomes to resist temptation. I elaborated on the subject by mentioning how that little voice inside my head had told me to get back in my car and drive off the night of my first DWI a year ago. A friend had followed me home after I'd refused to hand over my keys. In a fit of anger I raced home, managing to lose the person who had been following me. Once I pulled into my driveway and stepped out of the car, full of piss and vinegar glory for having ditched my concerned friend, I resolved that no one would tell me when and when not to drive. So in spite of the friend who was looking out for me, I hopped back in my car and barreled out of my driveway to enjoy a leisurely 3 in the morning cigarette on the road. I was pulled over for weaving, there was a case of empty beer cans in the back seat, I was tested, cuffed and stuffed into the cop car, taken down to the pokey and bailed out by my father. I blew sparingly into the Breathalyzer, which registered a 2.1 blood alcohol level on the Richter scale, so I was two times as drunk as a drunk driver gets pinned for, or close to blackout drunk. Driving While Intoxicated number one of two. We closed after I recounted my stupidity and I moved on to group therapy. At least I was honest in there.

After lunch I filled out fitness forms in order to use the gym, then I whipped off a vocational questionnaire. Everything here is very goal-oriented and positive. This place offers many options for emotional and physical self-betterment. The 'get well and high on life' method is powerful here.

My day was going well until I picked up a letter from my grandparents. 'Our oldest grandchild is in rehab!' I hate to even think about their reaction to the news. I was hoping that they would never have to know, but false hope sucks. The letter expressed complete support, addressing my problems subtly and in abstract ways to avoid such unpleasant words as 'rehabilitation clinic'. Now the doors are blown wide open. My nuclear family has extended the knowledge to every other living relative. This really blows.

Later in the lounge I sat with Pat the jailer. I explained my new and more potent 'victim of circumstance' story and got the feedback I wanted. Pat said, "We've all had our fun. Go out and do what you have to do in your college years. Just don't get your ass busted again." Yes! A friend who endorses my campaign and finally sees through my eyes. I mean come on, at least let me have some fun before I get out of college, all right? Just don't ever drive again!

I told Pat that I'm going to take this treatment program seriously so I can get the most out of it while I'm here. I'll take it easy and clean at least all summer. I'll go to the AA meetings, regain some strength and figure out what control means to me.

For some reason I've had something going on in the back of my mind that has told me that it would be all right to go back and party again for a couple of years once I'm out of here. This place is telling me quite the opposite, however. Why do I have to get into this kind of trouble at such an early stage of my life? I want to end my party years after college, not before. College will not be easy next year as it will be almost impossible not to drink. If I can't face it then I have to find an alternative, although I love my college and friends there. I have to bring this up in a group discussion before I explode because it's the hardest question I'm facing right now. Intolerable frustration. Help me!

Day 4 Wednesday, May 24

I ended last night's entry on a poor note.

Tonight the after dinner lecture was enlightening. Say the drunk's prayer and it stays easy, don't talk to the 'disease', the longer you are sober the more you love yourself, the importance of the 90/90 rule. The general sober man's rule is that one should go to a meeting a day for the first ninety days of recovery. The speaker said that in recovery we don't have to make any more promises. Surprisingly, this dried up gin bag made me feel like a million bucks in there.

The drunk's prayer is the prayer that a recovering person ought to say upon waking, throughout the day when necessary, and before bed. This is supposedly one of the most settling tools in recovery, the old drunk told us.

"God, please keep the desire to drink and drug from me this day."

I am noticing that in this program various concepts, terminologies and sayings resemble religious rituals. The abundance of recovery language creates its own universe. If nothing else, this field is a very interesting study.

Today was okay until I called my parents half an hour ago. Mom and Dad were clearly shattered and speechless over the phone. Mom sounded pessimistic and Dad told me that some of my college friends had called. "I'm sorry, college friend of my son's, but Sandy is indisposed for the next month. No, he's not enjoying the current rash of summer concerts... no, my oldest son is in rehab." I don't have the energy to deal with my friends because right now I'm only thinking about me.

Do you know where I could be and what I could be doing right now if I was not in this impossible mess of mine?

Day 5 Thursday, May 25

This morning I feel great as opposed to last night. Waking with a clear mind is very refreshing and new for me. My strength level has risen steadily and so have my spirits. You know how much I could accomplish if I didn't get wasted anymore? I read Aldous Huxley's *Brave New World* today, and it's the first book I've read cover to cover since I read Joseph Conrad's *Heart of Darkness* two years ago. I have been assigned a lot of books that I never got around to reading. I would just listen in class and bullshit my way into okay papers which were curved up in AP courses. I have not really completed a project since I started drinking heavily last year after my wrestling season ended, towards graduation, when students can get stupid like I did.

Today was Alumni Day. We had four of five meetings with alumni, listening to various stories and experiences from the inside and the outside. Each speaker has been clean and sober for over a year and they express happiness with their respective states of mind. I could relate to one speaker's suggestion that as an active addict, she had played a number of different roles in her life before the recovery process came into play. I mentioned the way in which I have also played different roles; athlete, burnout, drinker, honors student, ambulance driver, EMT, artist for local bands and the school paper. I developed a 'role repertoire' that allowed me to achieve the widest possible peer acceptance. This relieved social insecurities while allowing me to party with the most people and date some of the cool girls. In high school my best friends and I floated, social nomads in our little world, friends with everybody; the beach crowd, the popular crowd, the jocks, the burners, the geeks, the prep school kids, the ambulance corps group. We did what we wanted because we pretty much got along with everybody.

My family moved around when I was growing up, so I was always the new kid getting picked on when I changed towns or countries or schools. When this happens a lot you learn to defend yourself against bullies and you try to be nice to everyone. Maybe they will be nice back.

Widespread acceptance is comforting, although it can create confusion. I don't know if I could ever accept myself for who I was. Maybe I was trying to be everything to everyone. Maybe this is just the way high school is and I was looking at different things to figure out who I was. Where does that leave me? In rehab, where I can explore myself further.

We had an AA meeting with the alumni who spent the day with us yesterday. One of them is celebrating his 90th AA meeting in 90 consecutive days, the revered 90/90. The meeting was good. The following story gives me a ray of hope and reminds me that I'm not the only idiot out there.

At the ripe age of seventeen, Herb got drunk for his first time. His drunk friends accidentally dumped some harmful chemical into his eyes, which blinded him for three months. Later that year, after a basketball victory, he and his buddies went out to celebrate the joyful occasion. After he dropped his teammates off, Herb noticed an empty beer can lying on the passenger seat. When he hurled the can out of his window he accidentally hit the windshield of a passing police car. The two cops didn't like that so he spent a night in the holding tank down at the department and they towed his car.

Herb turned down several basketball scholarships because he thought college would not suit him. A year later he was an infantryman in Viet Nam. Several times he got drunk and was almost killed out of sheer stupidity by heavy enemy mortar fire. One morning, after a long drunken night, his patrolling platoon was ambushed and he was one of three survivors out of forty men. The three men spent all day walking back to camp, and Herb swore to himself that he would never drink again. He had a bullet lodged in his mid-section, so upon arrival he was rushed to the O.R. There was no anaesthetic so they gave him a bottle of Scotch that he guzzled down to dull the pain while the surgeon tore him open to find and extract the toxic bullet from his gut.

Once out of the hospital, Herb put a gun to his head because he couldn't take it anymore. The round misfired - the only round that misfired on him while he was in Viet Nam. After nine more months and two more bullet wounds he was finally sent back home with an honorable discharge and medals for his service.

Herb married and had four children. He drank on a daily basis, hiding his alcoholism by stashing bottles in the foliage around his yard. He always walked his dog as an excuse to fetch a quick drink or two, so his dog learned all of Herb's hiding places. One time, his wife walked the dog and the dog led her around the yard to all of his bottles. He said that he almost killed the dog for that but he didn't have the heart because he didn't want to hurt the children. Hiding bottles in the brush was no longer safe so he hid his liquor in the windshield washer fluid tank of his car, slurping on the windshield fluid hose in the garage every night while working on 'projects'. Once, when they were out in their new car for the day, Herb argued irrationally with his wife so he could go back to get his old car because it was Sunday and he couldn't buy a bottle. His wife had changed the fluid in his old car so when he took a big pull from the washer fluid he threw up in front of a shocked neighbor who was out watering her garden.

Eventually Herb's drinking resulted in a number of seizures that left him hospitalized for extended periods. Ultimately he made the decision to admit himself into a rehabilitation center, and his life has improved drastically since then.

Herb's skeptical, straight-faced narrative and occasionally pained expressions did us in. I was sitting with Randy, and the speaker had us rolling in hysterics from the beginning. I couldn't help but laugh in pity at this poor man's incredible misfortunes. At the same time I appreciated his excellent drunkalogue.

Day 7 Saturday, 27 May

Last night's discussion group began fine but soon we were all waging a verbal battle. It's the first time there has been screaming in one of my sessions. Discussion group is a daily, patient-run exercise. The community splits up into various groups depending upon the meeting or activity, and my discussion group is comprised of ten or so patients. A weekly elected individual serves as president, and a secretary is elected to take down the meeting's progress. A topic is chosen by the president each day and an hour long discussion ensues that is usually constructive and has helped me to gain significant insight into a number of issues that roll around inside my lumbering head.

Two days ago a new patient named Eugene joined and has done nothing but aggravate the group's progress. He's a massive slob, ignorant, rude, illiterate, old and set in his ways, from the hood, pissed. His former wife took pity on him and sent him here.

Our exercise last night was to rate ourselves from one to ten in terms of how we felt our recovery was going. I gave myself a five because several minutes before the discussion I had been struggling with the concept of three remaining sober years back at college. When it was Eugene's turn he said he felt great and gave himself a ten. This guy's a pile of shit, a complete brick wall with no regard or respect for anyone or anything. The group tried to get at his feelings but he continued to push us away, exclaiming repeatedly that he was on top of the world and had no problems. I got frustrated and told him that he was killing the spirit of the discussion. He immediately broke and screamed, "My father fought in the war for you! You could be my fucking son, you little whippersnapper! Ain't no twenty year old little shit gonna tell me what to do!" I wanted to pummel the son of a bitch. I hate his fucking guts.

At dinner Randy the wrestler said, "Eugene's renting free space in your head, so let it go." This concept makes sense and I have to embrace it in order to keep myself from strangling assholes like Eugene. I can't let that good-for-nothing screw me up in here. If he continues to destroy the morale of the group I will switch groups. We're all stubborn pricks in this place but this guy is too much.

Before bed last night I spoke with this guy named Nick about how he built his own company. I guess he can run his operation from here or from the mirror with a pile of blow on it in his bathroom at home. Small business fascinates me. If I could make it through college without drinking I'd have all those hours of useless party time to build something out of my best ideas. Do I want to be successful? Maybe it's time to get my act together and start working towards some serious goals like starting my own business. I can see this for myself and the rewards would be great.

Don left half an hour ago. He was a good roommate to have for my first week here. I hope my next roommate will be as cool as Don. Two other guys from my wing also leave today. They have been here a month so it's time for a change. People are always moving in and out of this place.

Group discussion was good this morning, surprisingly. Everyone settled down and I lost that angry feeling towards Eugene. He doesn't mean wrong, but I'm working hard, he doesn't care and his blind statements struck me personally yesterday. I realize that his behavior should not frustrate me. The only thing we as a group can do is attempt to help him. I shouldn't be angry just because I can't get through to him. It's not my problem, and his ignorance shouldn't take any of the positive energy out of me that I need for my own work.

Day 8 Sunday, May 28

Last night I started reading my second book. I used to enjoy reading and writing but I got bored of school years ago and this got worse my freshman year at college. In class I'd pick up on the plot and participate in the discussion as if I had read the material because I found the bullshit factor entertaining. That method becomes empty after awhile...sort of like my 19-year-old life.

Saturday evening entertainment followed dinner. People write skits, sing and do stuff like juggling acts. What the hell am I doing here? Pizza is a fringe benefit on the occasional Saturday night. During the festivities I talked to a new guy named Sal, a Colombian American, slight, wiry, five feet tall, a crop of jet black hair, a gold cross dangling low outside his panama shirt. Gritting his teeth, chewing on a plastic fork and conveying a cynicism darker than my own, Sal spoke candidly about the drug trade, running numbers, and his recent tattoo. "My girlfriend Maria," he opened his shirt and there on his heart she sat, greasy and red. Sal recounted the time he was chased and gunned down by three bullets during a failed drug transaction. He warned me that if I wasn't very careful, the same thing could happen to me. Uh, I don't fucking think so, Sal.

I called my parents and asked my father to bring some things up to me on their Monday visit. He can't believe that we are not allowed to wear shorts here, a rule to keep tight asses and pretty legs from interrupting our self-discovery in meetings. He also couldn't believe that we don't have free use of the tennis courts and soccer fields, as though this is a sports camp, as though these things exist here. We are locked up, we don't leave the building, the gym is small and indoors, we have limited access to a tiny deck on an interior courtyard for evening smokes. I told my father I felt like a caged animal, plucking at his heart strings for fun, and he was sympathetic.

I also spoke with my brother Matt for a few minutes. As always he was running out the door when I called. Where's your big brother, Matt? He's traveling with some friends, a brief and efficient white lie that is working when people ask about me this summer.

That recurring thought keeps plaguing me. Why did I get so drunk and drive home the night of my first DWI class? Why didn't I take the ride home that Walter offered me? Why did I have the bad luck to pass a cop? Why was I speeding when I passed the cop? And why couldn't I bullshit with the cop so he would let me go? Most significantly, why the fuck am I here?

If I didn't get another DWI I'd be set right now. I'd have a summer ahead of me, a job, money in my pocket, and I'd be chasing concerts around with my close friends or partying every night. Liquor and stupidity brought me here. Once I get out of this shithole I've got to do my best to salvage the remainder of the summer. It's all history now so I have to make the best of a raw deal.

When I check in with home these torments return.

Every time.

Day 9 Monday, May 29

After lunch I was paged to see my case manager Tina. She asked me why I was here, because from what she gathered there wasn't anything in my history besides a couple of DWI's that suggests I have a problem. Her sarcasm pissed me off. My blood test came back and I have an increased number of enzymes in my liver, which is a clear indication of heavy alcohol use, although at my age this is not severe. Great. She said that I've got a lot of work to do if I'm ever going to have a chance when I go back home.

Tina asked me about any possible family problems that I may have had in the past several years. I began by saying that my family was fine at first, but by the end of our discussion I was in tears and fuming at my parents. From what I've found, according to the 'Social Learning Theory', in order to create an 'All American apple pie' family image I was required to build an emotional wall to protect the family. Tina mentioned that dysfunctional doesn't necessarily mean bad or with negative intentions; it simply means that there may be some issues that aren't addressed in the healthiest ways. On the way out Tina shook my hand and told me that it was nice to finally 'meet' me, as though all of our previous meetings were bullshit and had amounted to nothing. In any case, her words intrigued me, and maybe she's right.

Once I walked out of Tina's office I felt completely rejuvenated. I've never talked about those emotions so a giant burden was lifted from my weary shoulders. I think I'll let my parents know how I feel when it comes time for the four day family session. I'll be damned if they pay no heed this time around.

I just spent the best two hours of my life with my parents during their visit. We talked about everything, and after the first several minutes our words lost their initial sense of awkwardness. We talked about how things are going and how I've come along since I got here a week ago. Matt and Christian are doing well. Christian, my seven-year-old brother, doesn't know about my situation as it will do him no good.

One of my best friends Walter recently told my father that last summer had been full of excessive drinking, that all of us were getting cocked. Walter explained to my father that we had all been stupid but that I had pulled the short straw by getting caught. I found this comforting because it suggests to my parents that I'm not the only college student who ever gets drunk, although I'm one of the unfortunate few who got tossed into rehab for being such an asshole.

Mom told me that one of my friends Sean, who coincidentally has been through rehab and is working on a year of sobriety now, is the ice cream truck man at all of Christian's baseball games. My mother told me that Sean goes to parties with his friends and has fun but he doesn't drink anymore. I ought to get in touch with him once I get out of here. Maybe we could eat some fucking ice cream and go to a meeting.

Last summer Sean got into a minor accident while he was drunk. He was arrested and went away to rehab. I remember sitting in lawn chairs at a friend's house one Saturday, drinking and smoking weed with a couple of friends. Sean had crashed his car the night before and was dropping by to pick up his sunglasses. I tried to coax him into partying with us, offering Sean a shot or a beer. He wouldn't give in and he left half an hour later. I was pissed off because he wouldn't join us. He didn't stoop to my level then, and he hasn't since. His story is inspiring.

I started rationalizing again today after my parents left

because I heard the cop who arrested me called the head of the ambulance service that I was a member of in high school. Since I spent many of my high school days driving or riding an ambulance and working at numerous emergency scenes, I got to know a lot of the cops, who were often on the other end of the stretcher I was carrying. We worked together and these bonds can allow for a bit of leniency here and there (for good reason with the hundreds of hours of service some people give to their community). The cop who arrested me told the head of the ambulance service that he was only doing his job. He actually said, "I'm sorry, I just didn't think he could have made it home."

If I had told the cop that it was going to be my second DWI and I might end up in jail for it, maybe he would have given me a break. Maybe I wouldn't be here if I had played my hand better. What a pisser! But I can't rationalize about this. I was so bombed I could barely get my registration out of the glove compartment, so there was nothing the guy could have done. I have to accept my present condition or I won't learn anything in here.

Another kid from my town named Charlie is here now. I've partied with him before but it's been a couple of years. He left high school for prep school. When I see him walking in those dreaded adolescent chain gangs he reminds me of my town and my past, which gets me thinking about the good times. Rationalizing is another way of saying that I'm remembering the good stuff about partying and forgetting the bad stuff, which is how people fall back into their nasty habits. I can't let the sight of an old face allow me to slide backwards.

Day 10 Tuesday, May 30

My new roommate Lonny doesn't smell that bad tonight. The next time I catch him not flushing or misfiring around the toilet bowl I'll kick his ass. I've had it with his twisted sense of hygiene. Stepping into the shower every morning and seeing a clump of pubic hairs the size of a golf ball makes me sick. The wind he passes has damaged my sense of smell. He clips his toenails and they spray all over the room while he's talking to me. Besides his primitive sense of hygiene and lack of manners he's all right. He can sleep through a fucking tornado with the drugs they put him on. Wherever I see him, whatever the occasion, the guy is fast asleep. Yesterday someone had to rescue him from drowning because he fell asleep in his split pea soup, blowing green bubbles all over his neighbors until someone saved him. He came back from lunch with split pea stains all over his shirt, which now hangs wet and wrung on my shower curtain rail. Right now he is out like a light on his bed with a towel over his face.

Last night Randy straightened me out pretty well. "It happened. Face it like a man and get on with things," he hammered me as we sat for dinner. I couldn't help but tell him about my fear of getting another DWI when I leave this place. He responded that I never have to worry about that any longer if I stay sober. Maybe I can become an athlete again. Randy spent the next twenty minutes explaining the best ways to build the body. He said that with the proper diet and workouts I could go from 175 to 195 pounds in six months. I like the idea so I began working out in the weight room with Randy today.

Group was really cool. We looked at my alcohol history, how it affected my life and we came up with grandiosity, perfectionism, anger, frustration, and lack of freedom. We discussed some of the problems I had at home. Alten suggested that I'm what they call an ACOA. ACOA stands for 'Adult Child Of Alcoholic'. My parents aren't heavy drinkers, so they are ACOA's as well because dysfunctional traits can filter down through generations. One of the dysfunctional traits I learned was that I was expected to make the family look happy and healthy for others, regardless of family tragedies that dented us hard along the way. The same goes for our nuclear family communication problems. A light went on here as I thought about family burdens in high school.

I thought I was never given the credit as a decent student and kid. I put a lot of pressure on myself in order to please my family but that never seemed to be enough. All I listened to or thought about centered around the mistakes I had made or would make. I started to feel isolated in my own home and eventually it became useless for me to fight back. I'll admit that I was never an angel, but I was a good kid, and the weight I felt during high school pushed me to the edge sometimes. I guess this is how adolescence can be. This may sound dramatic but I am trying to look clearly and honestly.

So I got a lot out of group today. It felt good to get things off my chest and I look forward to discovering more buried issues tomorrow. If this is my time to voice anger, fears and frustrations, I'll do it.

Day 11 Wednesday, May 31

I accomplish more in a day here than I did in a week my freshman year of college. I guess that ought to tell me something. When I get out of here I've got to concentrate on healthy activities in order to stay occupied and begin to feel a sense of accomplishment again.

I worked out between 3 and 4 pm. It feels good for the muscles to get tight again. I forgot all about the rush I get from working out, one of my past high school activities. I intend to continue this workout routine when I leave here.

I wrote my girlfriend Sarah today. We started dating a couple of months ago and we have had a nice time together. I talked to her before I came to rehab and we said we'd write to one another this summer because phone use is restricted. By now she's at her summer house and missed my first letter. I wonder if it could work out between us when I go back to school. Those spring days with her were special, although I was usually crippled by hangovers. I'm not sure how serious we should get at this point in my miserable life, but Sarah listens, we have fun, she is pretty and sweet and she cares about me, which feels really good.

My friend Ken sent me a letter. I was happy to hear from him. Ken, Walter and Brad send their best. I'm not missing much in town aside from drunken parties. Ken talked about going on a run of concerts this summer, one of my favorite things to do. I make shirts and posters, take off with the boys, sell my work in the parking lots to pay for concert tickets and extracurriculars, I experience some amazing music and another memorable adventure. This summer I am on an amazing adventure to rehab.

If I stay sober I'm going to be with my friends while I do it. In rehab they talk about losing old friends and bad habits, changing the scenery and people, but part of staying sober for me would be about maintaining my friendships with their passive support of my sobriety.

Day 12 Thursday, June 1

The first of June and here I am in good old rehab! I'm really sore from lifting weights in the past couple of days. That raw soreness, like the first week of a new season, is refreshing and feels great. I'll work the legs today and give my aching upper body a rest. Once the soreness goes away I'll start doing push-ups every morning and evening. I'm starting to eat a lot. I'm starting to love the taste of milk and salad again. In the next couple of months I can gain ten pounds of muscle if I work at it.

Eugene, that son of a bitch from my group discussion, went to the hospital last night because of some asthma problem. I think the fuck-wad bolted and this is the administration's bullshit story. I tried my hardest, but I always felt like punching his sorry ass out. I really hope that dickhead is gone for good. He's been the biggest thorn in my side since he got here and now he's not in my groups every day. Beautiful.

8:30pm. I was wrong about the Eugene. Randy told me he's coming back. Grant me the serenity to not strangle that shithead.

Today I met with my case manager Tina again and went back to the old rationalizing game that I've been working to tear myself away from, which is exhausting and only puts a damper on my progress. I expressed anger and frustration as Tina respectfully called me out on my bullshit throughout our meeting.

In group my therapist Alten tried to get at my hopeless rationalizations. The group agreed that a Breathalyzer reading of .26 clearly illustrates a high tolerance, as .10 or .08 is legally drunk in most states. I tried to accept that my victim of circumstance argument was just an escape. I got busted and that's the bottom line. Whether or not I got caught should no longer hang me up as this epitomizes the rationalizing mind. The fact that I can function (or fail) at such a high blood-alcohol level shows that I have a problem, whether I'm driving into a DWI or sitting on a couch watching a movie. As much as my brain knows this I fight the facts and the fight fills me with anger.

I have to put the past in the past and try to break down my emotional defense mechanisms. It's easier said than done because I'm so used to stuffing my feelings and shutting off when emotions come into the game. Bullshitting is prolonging my agony and complicating things. If I want progress I have to give up the past and use it as a helpful instrument to get better.

In fitness we did some jogging today. I still feel sore from the weights, but it's a healthy kind of sore. The workout is a time consumer here, where the clock crawls along, and the positive exertion of nervous energy is the best way to get it all out. I'm taking Randy's advice and eating more. Along with lacrosse and soccer, I wrestled in high school so I got used to eating ice cubes and lettuce for four months out of the year to make weight. When I was partying heavily off-season I stopped eating as booze is so caloric and I didn't want to turn into a fat piece of shit, so I turned into a skinny drunken piece of shit. I haven't eaten properly in a long time, so it feels good to eat well.

Day 13 Friday, June 2

Tina told me that I have to cut out the crap if I want to get healthy. From now on I can't waste brain power on the past. I have to concentrate on today. I can stick with this and recover if I stop rationalizing and minimizing. Drinking is a dead end for me and I don't have much to argue about there.

Last night one of the therapists lectured before our AA meeting. This therapist reinforced the simplicity of the program. He talked about how drunks and addicts complicate the easiest things. "It's so bloody simple," he exclaimed, "Just say the drunk's prayer every morning and evening. If you stay with that prayer, you'll never have to pick up again." I find it interesting how even in the strictest of programs every recovering individual has his or her own specific philosophy and adheres religiously to it. This particular therapist utilizes the drunk's prayer to instruct us, and his logic is persuasive. Imagine what an army of sober drunks could accomplish.

My new job is flag raiser. Every week we get a new task. I was B-wing kitchen man last week, which meant that I'd sponge the counter and keep the kitchenette clean. This week I march out into the morning sun and proudly raise the American flag. I've never hoisted a flag before. "Good morning America! Another glorious day of rehabilitation!"

There are seventeen detox patients getting ready to enter into the community, which means that I'm moving into the middle of the batch in terms of time spent here. When I was in detox there were no more than five of us and the lounge was a pleasant thing. I bet that old detox lounge has seen emptier days than today, with seventeen freshly sober, pissed off people looking for a seat and fighting over what channel to watch on the tube. It's a weird thing to work together with a bunch of stubborn, fucked up bullshit artists who are used to getting their own ways.

Some people come in after detox and are fine, some people come in and are still so twisted they tip the fragile balance and get packed right off to the hospital. Everyone cries all the time around here, but a few people really lose their shit right away and need the old rubber room. "I need a fix! I can't take it anymore! I am going to kill myself!", with all the theatrical posturing attached. One girl came in and left, same day service. In our community meetings that day she sat in tears, shaking like a leaf and looking like death while she told anybody who would listen that she had to get something into her system or she'd die. They quickly carted her off as she was freaking everyone out, which is hard to do to 75 drug addicts. One time, during a cocaine meeting slide show, a photo came up of two fresh eight balls of cocaine sitting on a mirror with a razor blade and a rolled up hundred dollar bill. Three people burst into tears and one had to leave the room. Although the physical detox shouldn't take more than seven days at most to get through, the emotional withdrawal from years of certain behavior can drive people apeshit. I didn't have DT's or sweats or anything when I quit drinking a couple days before I got here because I'm a young drunk, although I didn't sleep so well in the first week because I was deeply contemplating my alarming stupidity and shit-ass luck.

I started thinking about the promises I made to myself and others when my drinking gained momentum. Most of all I've let myself down. I'm a perfectionist, and since I always projected perfect results I was never happy with myself. I quit some things I never should have quit for this reason, like lacrosse my junior year when I didn't get a starting varsity position the first week of practice, which felt even worse. I need to refocus, work hard, never quit and accept the results.

There are two people who piss me off to no avail here, and I wonder if their only points in life are to test my patience. Eugene plagues my group therapy and discussion times. During physical activity a newcomer named Peter ticks me off. Ten or fifteen of us are there to relax, knock a volleyball around, and he starts cursing, arguing and telling everyone where to position themselves. He hobbles around with his synthetic motorcycle accident foot, talking pompous newscaster bullshit all day long. The little shit's a cameraman and acts like he's the prince of rehab. Everyone thinks he's an asshole except for the girl he's been hanging out with in the women's wing.

Aside from Eugene I had a constructive therapy session. I feel the beginnings of progress. I am now eager to get involved and look at the problems that have affected my life. If I can work these things out into the open I might one day be able to enjoy some sort of inner peace, which is only a dream to me now. My attitude has definitely changed since I was admitted. I am learning to take constructive criticism in positive ways, which is helping me to get a better picture of what I'm looking at. I need to be able to see before I can sort through all of these things.

Alten mentioned today that any time he asks about my family I throw up a protective wall and shut down. He said this suggests that I take a lot of blame in my family system, and some of that may not be mine to carry. We discussed the doormat issue and how I felt like a doormat any time I was at home. I'm still distant from this concept but I'll work on it. Family week begins on Sunday and I will be forced to throw some things on the table then. If I spill my guts next week we might be able to reshuffle the deck and deal the cards fairly again.

The Italian (as he refers to himself), the compulsive liar (as he refers to himself) and the cop leave tomorrow. They've all been good to me. I shook their hands and rubbed their coins for good luck.

I got the first letter from my girlfriend Sarah yesterday. She responded to my suggestion that I need time to straighten my life out. She wrote a caring letter in return. Her accommodating nature makes me feel guilty. She's been supportive, sweet and thoughtful. Letting go may be the best thing for both of us, but I find the urge to continue writing to her.

Here I sit in bed at rehab, about to get back to my book. Lonny, my revolting but friendly roommate, is snoring away on the floor because he couldn't make it to the bed. His new rule is that he can't touch his bed during the day because otherwise he wouldn't leave it. The man farts and snores and sleeps all day long. He is one crude act.

Day 14 Saturday, June 3

This morning I finished my book. I am remembering that I have to chip away at commitments every day in order to enjoy an overall sense of accomplishment. I lost that drive and motivation last year, so working on this might help me to feel whole again. Was I ever quite whole?

Tonight we had seventeen qualifying speakers in two meetings before and after dinner to get them all in. People come in waves around here. New faces filter in every day. I suppose that's what rehab is all about. They try their best to fix you up and off you go again. This place is like a factory where 5 to 10%

stay sober once they're out. The rehabs grease the stats but I don't blame them as there needs to be a healing receptacle for waste products, and someone has to make a buck on this business model in order to do it in the first place.

I spoke with my family about Family Four, which begins tomorrow. Family Four is four days of family group therapy. For the first time I realized something significant and consistent with my role-playing in the family. My brother Matt insinuated that the four day commitment was a sacrificial bummer, fishing for apologies, like I was wasting his time. My family has gotten used to me apologizing for them and to them and around them. I repeated several times to Matt, "that's tough, it's arranged and you're coming." When Matt realized that I was not going to apologize he hopped on the defensive and reiterated that it would all work out.

I am not a doormat. No one better expect extra praise or apologies for something they do for me that is part of this family. I got used to making a big deal out of a small helpful hand because I didn't want to burden my family. The phone conversation illustrates Matt being accustomed to getting an apology or praise from me when it's not warranted. If I'm part of a family I help out and I am helped in return. Right now I need some support. I'm afraid I have missed this point for several years. It's an important point to rediscover and work on.

Day 15 Sunday, June 4

Today was the beginning of Family Four. After morning group I spoke with my case manager Tina for half an hour. I told her that I'm ready for the next four days. Christian is only seven and therefore too young to benefit from or be traumatized by this marathon.

I told Tina how my family would take on some of my responsibilities without my knowledge, presumably so they would have more ammunition to argue that I was irresponsible and immature. Tina said that I was very loyal and defensive of the family, which is true. We discussed my shifting role from hero to scapegoat and how frustrating that had been for me. I mentioned how I got to a point where I expected nothing from any family member. Maybe I felt so much pressure that isolating myself gave me a false sense of independence. Ultimately, after a good deal of isolation, all my parents had left as leverage on me was the use of the car and the room that I slept in.

I think my parents took me for granted sometimes. I remember waking up at six in the morning the day before high school, heaving in pain with a massive stomach ache. My parents told me it was gas all day, and my mother gave me suppositories as a quick fix. They didn't know better, I suppose, but I could have used a doctor. They went to dinner and returned to find me shaking on the couch, 15 hours after I had complained about this damned stomach. Finally they took me to the E.R. "How long has your boy been in this condition?", the doctor asked. An intern came in and poked my arm full of holes, which prompted me to projectile vomit all over my mother. "Now his stomach is empty, we can operate immediately. Wheel him right in before his appendix bursts," the surgeon ordered. Meanwhile when Matt, who beat cancer at the age of 8, develops a mild sniffle, they rush him to the local doctor if not Memorial Sloan Kettering. I understand his history but why am I not able to see a doctor like Matt? Although this is an old example it's hard to ignore jarring contrasts in the way my parents treated us, at least on the medical front.

FAMILY GROUP

I sat with my family for an apprehensive lunch. Dad started needling me about the implications of a letter my best friend from college had written to the family in response to my situation, and I dropped the subject like a brick after suggesting that Dad was extending the words of a friend to fit his perception of me. I didn't want to get into irrelevant disputes with my father before we started.

As we moved to the lounge my mother explained how painful this was for her and how she had little to no hope for me. Matt looked on sympathetically. He still can't believe how unlucky I was to get a random, second DWI to initiate this mess. Dad spent his time craning his neck around to take in the lay of the land, people watching, checking out the competition.

The whole scenario struck me as absurd. The four of us sat huddled around a table, confused, awkward, disoriented. My parents exhibited textbook composure in extreme yet controlled circumstances. Matt mentioned the troubles he will have with his grades because of missing three days of class, at which point Dad requested that Matt not put us all on a guilt trip, which is something we're all good at doing to each other. Mom implied that my situation was reducing our family to rubble, that she would no longer live like this because she couldn't take it anymore. It came time for our preliminary separate sessions. I kissed Mom and told her that I would see them all later in the first family therapy session. As I walked away my mother started crying and I was filled with a sense of hopeless despair.

Later, five families sat in a large circle and introduced themselves. "Hi, my name is Sandy and I'm an alcoholic. It's hard to sit here with my family." The therapist asked family members how it sounded to hear their loved ones address themselves as alcoholics and addicts before speaking. Mom raised her hand and said that she felt shame and guilt. Several other people chimed in as Mom wept quietly in the background. Dad was embarrassed to be here, and Matt had an empathizing look on his face that read, "Why is my brother in this shithole?" I felt sorry for my brother.

A family tree exercise ensued and one family was used to illustrate the concept. The therapist's intention was to show how traits filter from one generation to the next, but she lost her audience in the details, going on for an hour and ending the day ineffectively. I'm still under the impression that there are alcoholics all over the place regardless of family traits and genes.

This evening I sat with Randy and an old Southern salesman in my wing by the name of Jake. Jake told us today that he had three different families in three different states for seventeen years. Kids and everything. None of his three families were aware that there was anyone else in his life. He split the week up, each week for seventeen years. His sales routes were designed around his families. This guy is too much. This is such deep deception that I wonder how he managed the time to become a heroin addict. I sat there with Randy and we peppered Jake with questions for an hour. He seemed amused by the attention. We couldn't believe this wingnut. He put his suitcase in the car, drove down the road to his next family, spent a couple days, then moved on to his third family, for two decades. There are a lot of liars in here but this guy had photos of each family and everything. Holy Shit Jake. What a disgraceful stud, what a heroic cad.

Day 16 Monday, June 5

After my 8am lecture I sat with my brother. Matt told me that Dad had sifted through my room and found a journal documenting the worst party experiences I could remember, a journal that sits at the end of an academic notebook from last semester along with a bunch of other book boxes in my closet. My father had been thorough and I was enraged at this shitty news, but I tried to keep a lid on it.

In our first family meeting at 10am I told the group that my best friends became my support system where I found love, loyalty, positive reinforcement, relaxation and good times that I no longer felt when I was with my family.

Matt told the group that he stayed away from home because when a fight broke out he wanted nothing to do with it. He said that he walked a fine line between my parents and me because both sides pressured him. He hated being in the middle all the time. He mentioned that the two of us talked a lot, related well, and he understood why I looked for a support system outside of our own home. He described himself as stable, competent, tough, independent, a survivor of cancer. He stays busy. He said that when he has problems he works them out himself because he doesn't want to depend on others. He said he doesn't like bullshit and he doesn't like people who quibble about unimportant things. His self-summation was fair, accurate and I liked his delivery as I always have.

The next activity got the whole room going. We discussed some of the most frustrating elements of our respective family systems and I hopped right in. One thing that angered me was that although my parents only talked about my mistakes to me, they liked to show me off because I looked good on paper and presented well. This confused me. I told the group that I was sick of playing the black sheep of the family and I was tired of feeling like a doormat. In going to college I enjoyed independence but I never felt quite whole as I had become an underachieving perfectionist. After years of feeling leaned on I no longer needed someone to pressure me because I had become my own hardest critic.

I continued on that I was hurting inside, that there was a lot of anger and pain. I explained that after some time I became indifferent and repressed feelings to avoid immediate and inevitable disputes with my parents. I clammed up and accepted any reprimanding words or punishment in order to get away from the problem faster, even if I didn't deserve it. Positive attention never was much of a factor in my house because my parents have utilized the more traditional negative reinforcement for years. The only way I felt noticed after a while was through negative attention, which sounds pathetic but is true. I knew somewhere deep down that I was good and that I tried, but those thoughts were often lost over the course of consistent criticism and self-punishment.

By this time I was in tears and the therapist brought my father into the discussion by asking what he thought of what I had just said. Dad replied that I was always sulking and brooding, much like I had during our greetings before the therapy session. I immediately shot out, "Do you know why?", and the counselor pushed me into answering my own question. I exclaimed, "Because Matt told me that you dug through my stuff and read the most personal journal entries I've ever written! What right do you have to do that to me?" My father fired back, "And what was all that writing about?", suggesting to the group that that the journal was a serious indication of my abuse. The therapist cornered my father by asking him if that was a fair question given the circumstances. Dad backed down for the first time that I can remember with a quiet no.

The whole group began to pile on about my father's lack of respect for my privacy. "What right do you have to do that? I never would do that to my children!", and, "How could you violate a loved one like that?" My father weakly responded to this barrage of questions by suggesting that he had simply stumbled upon the journal, although he'd gone searching through my closet with a fine-toothed comb. A wife of one of the patients stated strongly that to do such a thing was out of the question. The group stirred with discontent as I told the group I felt 'emotionally raped' by this situation, a term I spun and threw out there to stoke the flames. One of the family members suddenly let out a cry and spilled his guts about how he felt violated. He's here to support his father, but he completely related to me. The support and understanding from everyone made me feel much better. The conversation continued for a while, and by the end Dad was put in the spotlight like the jerk he'd been for doing this. He persuaded me to go to rehab and drove me here so what else does he want from me?

My father had no right to ask me what the journal was about, which was a last ditch attempt during group to keep the burner on me. But in this place everyone's fucked up, and now that we're working on things, morality issues and emotional issues take precedence over a few drinking or drug stories scribbled in a journal, which are batted around all day long in this place. Back at home he would have shoved this newfound knowledge down my throat at his leisure. "Well stay the hell out of my closet and personal belongings! Maybe one day you'll get the picture that respecting your son's privacy is part of a healthy family system!"

After we closed the meeting Mom came up and embraced me forever, uttering a stream of 'I love you's' into my ear. Dad felt foolish and tried to give me a hug but I was angry and shrugged him off. I ordered him to give the journal to Matt.

How can I gain my father's trust when I can't trust him?

Some good things happened in the family session. I don't remember the last time I let my emotions speak so fully, and I have never felt that kind of support for being honest with my family in my whole life.

After lunch, as I told Tina about my intense anger over the journal, I quickly got overheated. Tina asked, "Do you want to hold on to this anger for some reason? Do you think that holding on to this anger will help you in some way? Would you use it as a weapon?" I agreed with Tina. I have to let it out and let it go.

I went to group therapy before the afternoon family session. There are four new patients in group. Alten really 'pushed everyone's buttons' today, one of the terms used around this place. He left me alone after I spoke honestly but he was harder on the new guys who wouldn't share openly. He managed to break some more people down before the end of the meeting.

Watching people break down around me all day is a

new life. They're all tough and fuck you, digging their heels in, giving you that don't mess with me thousand yard stare. On the outside they'd kill you, beat you up, break your shit, steal your stuff, screw you back if you pushed them hard enough. But in here, seated in circles and talking about feelings with a tissue box in the middle, the nervous ticks come out, the subject comes close to home, and over time everyone breaks down. The flood drains out, the tears and the crying and the pain fall on the floor and it's part of this strange game, every day in this hallway of mirrors, looking at every angle of oneself. "Hey, you missed a spot... what about this way of looking at how twisted up you are?"

Family therapy followed group session. The therapist asked my father what he was thinking because he hadn't spoken once during the afternoon session. Dad became defensive, crossing his arms and legs, which are the only two things you can't do in group. So the therapist explained this and asked my father to uncross his defensive limbs while he said that he was 'fine'.

When the therapist opened the floor I said that I was angry and hurt because my father had read my journal. I spoke about the pressures and lack of trust I felt in my family. The therapist asked Dad to explain the relationship he had with his own father. Dad said his father didn't talk about feelings much. The group commented on the fact that I feel the same way about my father as he did about his father.

The therapist pretended to be me, and I was asked to act like my father. "Get to work! Stop wasting time! You don't care about anything! You'll never get into college! You scored two goals but you should have scored three!" I broke down and couldn't go on. It was awkward and a little campy, acting like my pissed off father in front of my family, but I felt a very intense and emotional release. I love my father and want a good relationship with him, but Dad seems to put himself beyond that as though it is his duty to be tough, stoic, remote.

Then I was asked to speak to Mom and I told her that I have always carried part of the burden of her sister's tragic death. Susie was nine months pregnant at the age of 24 when she was killed by a drunk driver on her way home from covering for one of her nurse friends at the hospital. The baby was delivered and lived for several minutes but they both died. The drunk driver never went to jail but our family should have hunted him down in my opinion. This was the first time I saw my father cry at the age of seven. His left elbow rested on the couch, his big hand covering his red face as he told Matt and me that Susie had died and gone to heaven so we would never be able to see her again. No more Susie smiles or back tickles, and the cousin we were going to play with went to heaven too that day. I told my mother that I was tired of carrying that burden, but for some reason I took some of the weight as if this might alleviate her heavy heart somehow. We cried as the meeting closed and hugged for a long time afterwards.

I've been thinking about that damn journal and only one thought makes me feel better. My father read about my worst experiences, so now there's nothing else to explain. There are no more secrets. It really sucks, but I am trying to accept the things I cannot change.

I WANT TO BE FRIENDS WITH MY DAD.

Day 17, Tuesday, June 6

Matt brought along the journal as requested. The journal was not as bad as I had remembered, although it wasn't the sort of thing I ever wanted to share with my parents. Dad's new evidence will reinforce his opinion that I am a mess and my DWI's weren't just bad luck. My Mom wouldn't read the journal because of the privacy issue and perhaps more importantly because she knew it would have made her hysterical.

I wrote this journal during a one week suspension in January as a result of the 'Wrong Room Incident'. My suspension in retrospect was a comic misfortune fit for a drunken fool. Late one night in a blackout apparently I stumbled home to the safety of my dorm. I walked up the stairs, turned left to where my room was, but I had walked up one extra flight of stairs to the third floor of my dormitory in a wasted haze. I punched in the combination of what I thought to be my dorm room. The numbers I punched into the combo lock miraculously opened the door. This would have been my door had it been on the second floor, so it was a gallant effort to get home. I walked in blind drunk and flopped down on the floor futon as this happened to mirror the exact layout of my dorm room. The girl whose room I had mistaken for my own was at first alarmed, then annoyed. She tried unsuccessfully to rouse me and send me on my way. In fluent drunkenese I allegedly told her that this was my room, I asked her to please leave, let me have some peace and quiet so I could get some shuteye, at which point I yanked the comforter away from her and over my head, turned away, passed loud wind in her direction and began to snore. Discouraged, the girl alerted the resident assistant. The RA managed to squeak my name out of me before I suddenly got up and walked out of the room after he'd harassed me long enough. Then he found my name and picture in the freshman photo book. I woke up in my room. The lights were on, the door was wide open and I had no recollection of what had happened until I was notified of my suspension by the Resident Director that day. After a week's suspension I went to the Student Council with my architectural diagram of the dormitory and I made my innocence quite clear in the case of 'The Wrong Room, Wrong Floor Incident'. The girl testified on my behalf that there was no malicious intent whatsoever, that the episode after the initial fright was in retrospect a humorous misunderstanding involving her room and a disoriented drunk. The issue was also raised about the marginal quality of the combination locks, why any number combination would open a door randomly. The case was dismissed and I was immediately reinstated, but damage had been done on the home front as my parents had been notified.

During my suspension period I was not to set foot on campus, which meant that I was forced into refugee status. I went over to another dorm and spent a week in a room of my two good friends, sleeping on their couch and writing all day. They would bring me food and the bathroom was right next door, so the ordeal worked itself out without my having to return home. The writing I did during that scared, confused week illustrated the absolute dregs of my party experiences. I wrote about the sacrifice, the endurance, the pain and emptiness involved in this sort of lifestyle. I spent hours recapping my most abusive and extreme times as a waste product, seemingly as an act of desperation and therapy. The writing was real and did not glorify my activities as a chemical warrior. During that week I poured my life into the journal that my father found the other day. I remember the shocked responses of my friends whose room I hid out in when I read them several passages and they couldn't relate to the extremity of my mind set. Granted, they're girls and more moderate than me, but if my friends had trouble relating to these stories my Dad probably thinks I'm a fucking wacko by now. Well, what's the use worrying about what is no longer hidden? Maybe I should write a book about all of this for the next one of me out there.

Family session ensued after my morning lecture. The group formulated a human sculpture from one of the families in the session by moving them around in the center of the circle until their arrangement seemed to match their family state. Then everyone elaborated on the concepts behind the exercise. We could all identify with this activity, and the group seemed more collected and satisfied with the concept of family therapy after two trying days of emotional work.

Towards the end of the morning session the therapist worked on my family for a bit. When asked to talk about his feelings, Matt became defensive and offered his philosophy on life, which includes dulling emotions to deal with this shitty week. The therapist requested that he share his feelings, but Matt is not interested in falling under this particular microscope and I don't blame him. He said that he always felt pressure from both sides because the communication between my parents and I had become virtually nonexistent. He told the group that he was sick of being the mediator between two opposing parties under one roof. I understood his difficult position.

The therapist asked Dad how he felt. My father said that my words yesterday were essentially full of shit. This was great because he was silenced by the group again and made to listen. When Dad started speaking the symptomatic language of 'I should have done this, I should have done that', the therapist explained that there was no need for defensive posturing. The therapist went on to tell my father, "What your son says is real because that's how he feels, and it seems that he was not properly heard, judging by your defensive position." Just try to listen to me, Dad.

Mom apologized and told me that she never meant to hurt me. She said that she loved me and just wanted to see me healthy. I told my mother that our relationship was a two-way street, that I had caused heartache in the family with my self-destructive behavior, but I reiterated that I had trouble throughout high school because I always felt like I was up against a wall with my folks as the pressure heated up.

The therapist then asked me how I thought my parents' marriage was. I said that my parents are very strong and have grown accustomed to working through a lot of difficult times because of their unconditional love and dedication to the family and to one another. When there was a problem to confront, my parents got together and fought it as a team, which carried over into the times when they had to deal with me. Their bond and efficiency as a team made it difficult when I conflicted with them because they were unwavering in their strengths and beliefs, I suggested. Perhaps since they had grown so accustomed to managing one family tragedy after another I subconsciously found negative attention here and used it as a tool to achieve some feeling of love and security. The session went very well. I hugged my family at the end of the hour and they were off until tomorrow.

Group therapy at 1:30pm was interesting. Several newcomers told their stories to the rest of our small group. I'm getting much better at analyzing bits and pieces of dialogue. I've learned that there are motives and emotions behind all the words. It is stimulating to look at the dynamics of recovery from an academic angle. When I hear the bullshit that comes from the mouths of new patients I realize how much I've developed. It now makes sense to me that the therapists concentrate on breaking down the emotional makeup of a patient in order to build new and healthier attitudes which are more conducive to recovery. When I got here I was in the same frame of mind as the newcomers I heard today. I heard rationalizations, minimizations, blatant denials, generalizations, apologies. I saw defensive posturing, crossed arms and legs, angry eyes hiding fear. People have to scrap these useless things fast if they really want to get better.

Day 18 Wednesday, June 7

Martin is in my morning men's group, a quiet, slight waif with mousey, thinning, strawberry blonde hair and a matching moustache. After two weeks of silence he started talking. He's in here for blow and drinking like a lot of people. One time he picked up a hooker and they went to a family cabin on a lake, near the city he lives in. She gave him a blow job and then started to strip. It turned out that she was a guy when Martin saw the hooker's big hairy balls. The group was incredulous. Nathan asked if Martin kicked the guy's ass, which Nathan would have done, and Ray asked if he shot the hooker, which is what Ray would have done. Martin didn't know what to do, and the hooker was bigger than him. He wasn't going to get his ass kicked by a hooker, so he dropped the hooker back off on the street corner and paid the fucking hooker. Holy shit. The group was very supportive. We all felt sorry for this poor bastard. Ray crossed his arms, leaned back in his chair with the trademark toothpick between his two front teeth, and said smoothly, "I would have killed that motherfucker."

There's an old vet across the hall from me named Frank. He's been here a week and he keeps walking into random rooms trying to find his own, sometimes half naked. He has trouble dressing himself, he is disoriented, he can't remember anyone's name, when his sessions are, where the dining area is. I just saw him wander out of his bathroom, naked from the waist down, holding a dirty pamper and wondering what to do, so I called down the hall for someone. This poor guy has wet brain and he's so far gone I don't know how they can help him at this point.

Day 19 Thursday, June 8

The one-on-one part of family recovery kicked off the day. Mom talked about how she always took on every family problem as though it were her own fault. She suggested that her feelings may have been connected to her old family system. She felt the pressures of being the only one in her family to stand up to her father, and she said that she was familiar with the doormat concept as well.

Dad became a little emotional when he talked about his father and how his father may have been a heavy drinker on occasion. I remember him as a loving grandfather, but I was a grandson and not a son. Dad said that his father gave orders and didn't support the family emotionally sometimes. It wasn't until the age of thirty that Dad felt like he had become friends with his father. I told Dad that I just wanted to be friends with him and that I could identify with what he had said about his own father.

I remember when my grandfather died three years ago. I got home from school and I walked in to see my father sitting in his chair in the den. I said a meager hello and went up the stairs to my room without telling him I was sorry to hear that his father had died. We had been having a tough time, clawing at each other, and I didn't know what to say, so I said nothing. My father came into my room several minutes later and asked, "My father died today and you can't say anything to me? You can't even say you're sorry to hear about my father? What's wrong with you?" He was angry and upset, he stated his case and walked out of my bedroom. I pulled out a sheet of paper and did a sketch of Gunny, my grandfather, who I had always loved, who had been an excellent grandfather to me. I felt guilty as hell that I didn't have the balls or compassion to tell my father I was sorry to hear about his father's death. I just didn't know what to say. I learned then that acknowledging Dad's pain, just saying something, would have been better than saying nothing at all. My Mom told me about how she would see people at the grocery store and many people would not acknowledge that her sister had just been killed or that Matt had cancer when he was fighting it, talking about the weather instead of being human and saying simply, "I'm very sorry for your loss," or, "I am very sorry for your troubles."

We all talked about how my parents have been so strong and had to go through a lot of difficult things together, and how love and dedication has kept them together. They talked about Matt's bout with cancer in 1980, which immediately brought the family back to New York City from London, where we had been living for two years. My parents thought Matt's treatment was very difficult for me like it was for everyone in the family. Matt took it like a survivor at the ripe age of eight. They never told me Matt had cancer until cancer had been blasted out of his body, so I felt completely out of the loop. I said that this made me feel less significant so I resolved at the age of ten to become independent emotionally. I mentioned that Matt was rushed to the emergency room when he had the sniffles while I agonized in a fetal position all day when I was fourteen because my appendix was on the verge of exploding. "You'll be fine, son." I never felt heard or understood, so I stopped trying because it never seemed to make a difference. The one-on-one session ended with Mom and Dad's pledge to continue going to Al-Anon meetings, which are designed to help the loved ones of alcoholics.

The last session with all the families was a recap and summary of four intense days. I concluded by saying that all I hoped for was love and support from my parents. The meeting ended, we said goodbye and my family departed.

Day 20 Friday, June 9

I can't fucking believe this.

Tina just told me that the therapists have recommended a halfway house for my continued recovery. That really pisses me off, but now that I think about it I'm almost certain that every young adult is given this recommendation. Shit. That just threw me way off course. I've just got to put this bad news to the side and concentrate on the program. When I get out of here I'm going home to start fresh, and that's final. The program has wedged its way into my stubborn head, and I will learn to work on it when I'm back on the outside. This summer can still be lots of fun if I do it right.

Alten followed up on Tina's message by explaining how fantastic a halfway house would be for me. He mentioned how I gather my thoughts in writing and if I were to go to a halfway house I might even write a book about it. I would like to write but I would prefer to do that in the privacy of my own fucking home. They are pounding me with this halfway house concept, it's freaking me out so I just have to let it roll off my back.

No one showed up to speak at our 8 pm lecture and the staff was not aware of this so the community tried to run its own meeting. This was funny. The subject of respect emerged as the meeting topic. Everyone promptly did away with respect and started cross talking, character sniping, arguing with one another. A bold soul would scream, "Shut the hell up everybody!", the meeting would settle down for a minute only to ramp up again. One of the patients, an old oaf who has resided here in seclusion for the past month, contributed by saying he was here for himself, so if he wanted to sit in a 'fucking' corner and read the AA Big Book then that's what he would do. After being in ten rehabs and five halfway houses, the man has some seniority and his assertion couldn't easily be silenced. The community became panic-stricken. 'Oh no, he wants to isolate!' Sweaty palms flew in the air until the commotion began again. Eugene stood up and exclaimed, "Fuck this!", then proceeded to the back of the room to sit in the corner. "He just divorced himself from the community! What do we do now?" people shrilled. Some patients began to cry while Randy and I started laughing. I felt like I was a Ken Kesey character in *One Flew Over The Cuckoo's Nest*. Chief, throw the sink through the window so we can skip out of here before they lobotomize me.

Day 21 Saturday, June 10

In discussion group each person talked about what he would do if he only had a year left to live. I said I would spend the last year of my life creating art that would live in museums.

I just finished qualifying, or speaking about my history from the podium as a parting statement to the entire community of 80 people. I talked about how the first time I drank I pounded a six-pack of beer in 43 minutes on New Year's Eve and threw that up three hours later at the stroke of midnight when I was thirteen. I talked about my progression, the trouble I got into, the blurred life I have been living for a year, why this place was good for me and so on. I stared at the Preamble plastered to the dais and didn't look at my audience once. I was afraid I might freeze up or catch sight of Randy, who would have made me laugh myself off the stage, so I kept my eyes down. I was nervous as hell but I got through it.

After the meeting I spoke with a new patient named Jim about LSD. This guy remembers when LSD first came out and was sold over the counter in head shops before Uncle Sam made it illegal. We talked about how once you've been there you don't really need anything else. Acid was fun, dangerous, cheap and you never knew what sort of a trip you'd be taking. One time Jim dropped these orange barrels at a Poconos festival and his trip lasted for three days. I remember that some people were doing coke my junior prom, but cocaine was expensive and I was afraid of that drug at the time, so I popped three purple barrels to be safe, a synthetic mescaline type of high. The party ended at dawn, everyone went home and I spent the next 15 hours rolling around by myself on the beach, waiting for the buzz to wear off. Yeah, that's normal.

Grateful Dead concerts drew 100,000 fans and some of the heaviest hallucinogens known to mankind. People walked around saying, 'Two for five,' or two hits of liquid acid for five bucks. What a bargain. A fifteen hour brain dart for the cost of a stadium pretzel. I would pay the guy and he would squeeze two drops onto the backside of my hand between my thumb and forefinger. "Have a nice trip," he would say while I lapped it up. I never knew what I was sampling so this was half the fun, the anticipation, wondering just what sort of trip I was going to be off on. Coke was a hundred bucks a gram, which equated to many hours of landscaping for me at the time, so that was for friends with large allowances who liked this buzz. I never really got into cocaine as a popular national campaign scared me away from that cost-prohibitive powder. Acid was so heavy that I didn't want to do this stuff all the time either. I may have been a drunk for a year or two but I did not want to turn into one of those crispy critters I'd see scampering around the parking lots at Dead shows, wigged for life, the darks of their eyes dropped out, walking in circles with their brains pinned to the floor. This reminds me of the guy who jumped into a swimming pool with a sheet of acid in his shorts, which soaked into his leg and put him in a rubber room where he could spend the remainder of his existence trying to convince the hospital staff that he was a glass of orange juice. I remember one time at Saratoga when I was given what I thought was two hits of acid. I popped them in my mouth to my friend's dismay, who quickly explained that I had just popped eight hits of acid instead of two. I remember apologizing profusely as my three friends looked on. I replaced their hits but that's not what worried them. They were imagining how screwed I might be with eight hits of acid in my head. The trip was dirty and weird, but I got through it without losing my shit and drove half the way home after the concert. As a matter of fact the drive home was a peachy cakewalk. On the sunny, perfect condition highway drive up to Saratoga, the car I was in the back seat of did a 540 degree spinout, it's rear bumper gently kissing the guard rail overlooking a cliff while three eighteen-wheelers bore down on us, swerving and brakes smoking with all their might to avoid crushing our car. Not a scratch and we all could have been goners right there. Now that was a trip.

Day 22 Monday, June 12

We have a new therapist named Franz, who was effective today. He tested the group out, pushed some buttons, and managed to get under the skin of some of the people in our session. It's difficult when a therapist picks you out and starts pressing you. You're alone and vulnerable, and if you're hiding something it's hard to hold tight with a therapist who knows all the right cards to play. As I've worked through many of my problems here the pressure decreases consistently because now I am ready for criticism and I'm honest. Therapy is much easier if you are honest because you don't have to concentrate on hiding things and bullshitting bullshitters. When I got here I was pressured twenty-four hours a day until I began to open up. Once I let it all hang out I learned how to look inwardly and actually help the group as I searched for answers with them. The individual in denial has all the answers to justify his false sense of reality, so the breaking of those emotional barriers is hard. The walls are knocked down and a new foundation is poured with healthy knowledge. Most people don't get there. Most people pick up their old habits soon after they leave this place, but if a therapist reaches one person he's doing his job, or so they say.

Tina hunted me down again about the halfway house and I continued to push back. When I left her office I felt unsteady and confused about the whole thing. How can I convince everyone that I don't need a damn halfway house?

I got a joint letter from my buddies today and suddenly longed to be with my best friends. I sank into a temporary depression, thinking about the prospects of continued torture at a halfway house. Just my luck, when everyone else in the world is having a ball. My head became stronger at dinner however, and I was surprised by my emotional recovery. Here I am sitting on the old pity pot and slowly... no, quickly, some ideas slap me in the face and whammo, I'm out of the self-pity rut. I started thinking positively about going home with my recovery, and my thinking straightened out. During the evening meeting I started feeling really good again. When I keep the past out of the picture I don't beat myself up and I feel peace.

Day 24 Tuesday, June 13

I plan to go home and stay sober because I have the knowledge and the drive now to do so. I've got a brain on my shoulders, and I know that whatever the hell anyone says, a halfway house is not the right thing for me.

I dropped off some exercises that Tina gave me yesterday. She is itching to get on the horn with my parents about the halfway house. The whole therapy department wants to send me away for continued treatment. "Ah, here it is in the therapist's rule book. Please turn to regulation number 38." They really have the ability to railroad you. There is no way I should have to pick watermelons for minimum wage at some shitty ranch for three months. What the fuck! Well, that will be settled today because I'm standing up for myself.

Before group therapy I got a constructive staffing session by Tina, Alten and two other therapists. They opened up my mind again to the possibilities of continuing recovery in a less structured atmosphere. They want to ship me off to Arizona for the summer. I have to admit that they had a lot of good points, and I was forced to think twice about my hasty decision to reject the halfway house idea. They made sure I understood that if I do not go to a halfway house they will not give me a 'Therapeutic Discharge', which is the legal clean bill of health that I need to wave at the DWI judge in order to avoid extended community service or jail time. The therapists were firm, down to earth, and they displayed caring concern. I took the news without flinching, although it sucked.

To be honest with myself, I can't think of negatives aside from the fact that I don't want to go away for another three months, which means that I would miss the fall semester. This is a killer. It makes me feel like a failure, outside of the four year track that my parents believe is the proper way to finish college.

The more I consider it, I should have no reservations about the halfway house. I will miss my friends but nothing will change. What are all my friends going to do when they realize that life is not just one big party? I guess reality sinks in after school. I wonder why I have to do my harsh reality with three years left of college.

What about concerts, traveling, women, the remaining temptations that flood my mind? I have to let them all go. My job right now is to get sober and stay that way. I need to continue my recovery, and a halfway house might be the best thing for me. I can sit around all day and argue that I don't need any more help, but where will that get me? What does it matter anyway? It's time for me to make a responsible decision for once, and I think I've made it.

Day 25 Wednesday, June 14

I just got my discharge physical. Three days and I'm outta here. Out of here and off to Arizona, that is. Tina paged me away from group therapy this morning and I walked in to see three therapists with Mom and Dad, who sat nervously but patiently. I was shocked as all hell but I muted my astonishment as I took the last remaining seat across from Tina's desk.

Tina began to explain her reasons for calling my parents to 'join us' today. When she asked me how I felt I told the room that I felt awkward and angry. She continued by restating some of the issues the therapists covered with me yesterday, underlining the importance of continuing treatment. Everything she said made perfect sense, however much I hated hearing it. Yes, in fact it was true that there were no negatives in going on to a halfway house for three more months. I responded by saying, "Well, I already decided that I'm going, so it wasn't necessary to bring my parents all the way up here for this." My parents seemed completely relieved and the meeting closed immediately after my rapidly uttered words. I think they were all ready for a showdown, but the best thing to do in a no-win situation is to readily admit defeat. The only way for me to save any face was to tell the group that I'd actually decided to go on to the halfway house the evening before on my own, so the family intervention was just a big waste of time.

I proceeded out to the dining room and sat with my parents. I leave on Monday and I will spend ninety days at a halfway house Tina has arranged for me. The place is coed and there are thirty or so residents at any given time. Some of my rehab mates are there now so I will join them.

Mom brought up a photo album that shows my growth

from a baby into a young adult. I looked at my childhood and remembered running around carefree with my brother on the endless fields, kicking a soccer ball, joking, laughing, full of life.

We made a list of the things Mom and Dad should bring on Sunday when they visit for the last time before my departure. Mom started to cry and we all said we loved each other. I gave them both a hug and said goodbye until Sunday.

It's time for me to do some things for myself now. I've begun the process. Good things will come if I continue to work hard. My new life is only beginning.

Day 26 Thursday, June 15

Today is the 21st anniversary of Mom and Dad's wedding day. I love them very much.

A group of outside people came to talk to us tonight. On their way here a car flipped off the road in front of them into a large pond. The speaking group pulled over and they all dove in to rescue the driver and his two passengers. The people in the submerged car were all shitfaced. This group saved a couple of lives then came to speak, their clothes soaking wet with pond water and blood stains, talking up a storm, buzzed up on the adrenaline of saving lives that I got used to when I drove an ambulance in high school for the town's ambulance service.

It was my turn to sit at the head of the room for the community meeting. Words of inspiration and support echoed out. Follow up with your art, write a book, you're on the right track so work it and you will be all right. It was nice to feel like these people cared about me enough to give me some good energy. After the community spoke I read a poem I found.

THE MAN IN THE GLASS

When you get what you want
In your struggle for self
And the world makes you king for a day
Just go to the mirror and look at yourself
And see what that man has to say
For it isn't your father or mother or wife
Whose judgment upon you must pass:
The fellow whose verdict counts most in your life
Is the one staring back from the glass.
Some people may think you a straight-shooting chum
And call you a wonderful guy
But the man in the glass says you're only a bum
If you can't look him straight in the eye
He's the fellow to please, never mind all the rest
For he's with you clear to the end
And you've passed your most difficult test
If the man in the glass is your friend
You may fool the whole world
Down the pathway of lies
And get pats on the back as you pass
But your final reward will be heartache and tears
If you've cheated the man in the glass

-Author Unknown-

The poem is sentimental and a little schmaltzy but the message is insightful and worked over a couple people in the audience, whose tear mains broke. We capped the meeting and I returned to my room satisfied.

I've come a long way and I feel pretty good as Arizona seems like the best thing for me today. I just have to hold my head up and I will get through it.

Day 27 Friday, June 16

In the shower between meetings I began to think about how typical the night of my last DWI had been for me in the past year.

I got to a point where I was never quite satisfied with the amount of booze I consumed until I was blacked out. When there was a lot to drink, I always felt like I had to be one of the major contributors in polishing off whatever the party offered. I would find myself in a one-on-one situation with the keg or the bottle, battling with a flailing keg tap as though it were a serpent rising from the stormy depths. I never won, of course, unless passing out is winning. If I didn't have a beer or a cigarette in my hand I didn't know what to do with myself. On those occasional nights when I remembered walking or driving home I would be pissed off because this meant the parties had run out of booze before I had achieved the state of oblivion that I had gotten hooked on.

So I get to the party and my eyes light up, not as much from seeing old high school friends but from seeing one of those barrels packed in ice and tenderly cared for. Hey Jim, how are you doing Sally, how is college life? Sure, me too, where are the cups please?

I decide to start off with a bang so my goal is a six pack in half an hour to get the ball rolling. The next beer is the foremost thought in my mind throughout the evening, and it's always an escape. Oh, excuse me while I get another drink. Everyone is socializing but I can't focus for five minutes because my thoughts are on the next beer. "What did you do today? How was work?" And now let's get down and dirty. I drink too fast to enjoy the pleasant buzz of several beers. I always feel fine until suddenly I'm completely wasted, I go on auto pilot and then the morning.

Time to pick up a pack of butts and head to the next party at one of my favorite places in the world, a best friend's home on Long Island Sound. I breathe in the saltwater air as I wander down to rest on the tailgate, which is backed up to the beach. I've found myself here a hundred times, gazing red, burning eyes into the light of the dancing fire without a care in the world, music coating the landscape and skipping off the summer water. I am held up like a book by bookends, a friend on either side. My friend Cathy is good to lean on and we joke around while swaying casually to the music. I am peacefully numb again. I have accomplished my mission for the evening, and my memory begins to fade.

That's the last thing I remember before getting a DWI that night when I look back at Monday, May 14, my last drunk... and I blew a 2.6, which I think is legally dead in some states.

Before my group meeting I called home and talked to Matt. Last night he had some buddies over, and more than expected showed up. As he was shoving everyone out the door our parents came home and were pissed off to find the remnants of this small party. Today when Mom was cleaning out Matt's closet she found a beer can, which Matt said had been mine. This was not my beer can and this is the last time I am taking on that crap.

When Matt gets in trouble, my parents usually think, 'Well, this is nothing like the time when his older brother did something worse', so he often gets away with a slap on the wrist. He's also a good kid and doesn't push it like I did with our very strict parents. Now that I'm no longer around to be the bad example comparison model, Matt doesn't like the new heat that I am familiar with.

I don't know why but it feels like my brother is blaming me for stuff I have nothing to do with, like that beer can. I'm sick of family guilt drifting my way. This is not a mirage. This blame and guilt actually float my way like a magnet. I'm tired of playing scapegoat and I won't take it anymore. The family doesn't have a dumping ground in me any longer.

I am realizing that my town gets on quite well without me. I hope that my best friends take a minute to remember that I'm gone and send good thoughts. I'm off to Arizona now and nothing from my old life will change except for me if I stay strong.

Day 28 Saturday, June 17

At the community picnic I sat with Randy and some of the other comedians as we took turns laughing our asses off. I'm learning to laugh again without the booze. I'll miss Randy, the laughter, the games. He has become a close friend and a little like a big brother. I wish him the best when he gets out of here.

The evening rolled in and Saturday entertainment was fun. Towards the end everyone started singing "We Are the World", which was sappy but moving. When the night closed people bid farewell to those of us who will be leaving Monday.

It turns out that I will be going to Arizona with Dell, a mid-twenties prep with a nice watch, loafers, a golf tan and a deep, cynical humor paired with an earnestness I respect. He's very good at recounting his hard party experiences, so we have traded amusing stories over the past several weeks. I like Dell, we get along, we make each other laugh, so it will be good to fly out there with someone else from rehab.

Day 29 Sunday, June 18

I spent the day talking to several counselors and the community about my departure. Someone is always leaving from this place every day. Now it's my turn.

I went in to see Tina between meetings. She said that I am beginning to develop a decent understanding of myself and that my self-awareness will grow along the way. She mentioned that my presence is strong, I demand respect in unspoken ways and that this can serve me well as I continue to get better.

I went over my relapse issues with Tina. She thinks the control issue is probably the most prominent thing I have to keep an eye on. I told her that my decision to go to Arizona was a breakthrough. By letting go I was able to distinguish my wants from my needs and I realized that Arizona was the best thing for me to do.

The moment I made the right decision to venture West for extended recovery a strange euphoria lifted my spirits as shame and guilt were swept away. These burdens have lingered inside me for a long time so this feeling of release was notable. I sensed an uncommon band of trust form when I spoke with Mom and Dad the day I agreed to go to Arizona, something I have not felt in several years. Our honest and open dialogue was a first and I want more of it.

It seems like the decision to go to Arizona broke the spell of the scapegoat complex. I feel at ease and confident now because I am helping myself, and in helping myself I am making amends to the family. I have admitted my faults in hopes that my life can and will change, whatever the costs will be. Negative parental attention has given way to family support and positive attention. I have wanted nothing more from my parents, and I'm finally starting to feel the love I've needed or thought I was missing.

In the past several years many family problems have been thrown on the back burner to deal with me, or so it feels. Once this pattern developed, it was ingrained into the family system and I became the scapegoat. In one way or another I took on the burden of every negative aspect of the family that drifted into the household. This was a heavy weight and a confusing dynamic to walk with.

Matt is feeling restless about these developments, however happy he may be that I'm trying to get my head screwed on right. He will have to work with our parents directly now that his big brother, the family shield, has been removed from the equation. When Matt had a problem, which never compared to mine, our parents let him slide and ended up shaking their heads in my direction. Comparisons stirred old sediments and a constant rehashing of my faults and old mistakes. Now that I'm trying to get better it's not right for me to be compared to or used like this. Unresolved problems won't linger in the closet at home anymore. There is no longer any excuse to throw problems on the back burner or turn in my direction. Things are changing for the better and I feel these changes.

For a while I really began to think that it was essential for me to be around in order to take everyone's crap, as though this was a normal thing. Extremes become norms to the troubled individual in family patterning, which accounts for those past sentiments. I've learned that my family can get healthier with me, they will work with me on this, and it feels very good to know that. Other people are not so lucky.

I want to learn how to become a strong individual in the next few months, something I've dreamed about for a long time. In Arizona there won't be outside pressure on me to conform to the ideals of others. I would like to find myself out there.

Day 30 Monday, June 19

Last night after packing the community members signed my AA book. I was pretty exhausted and slept hard. This morning Tina gave me the folder with all of my work and I gave her a hug for good luck. She's been great. Everyone here has been great for that matter. I feel like the staff really cares about what they do. They helped me.

It was good to get my confiscated belongings back. I shook some hands and walked out into the morning wearing shorts, a hat and a tee shirt. It's nice to wear shorts and a hat again as these things were restricted in rehab. The facility vehicle rolled up, I got in with Dell and we rode off into the sunrise.

3

The Mesa Halfstep

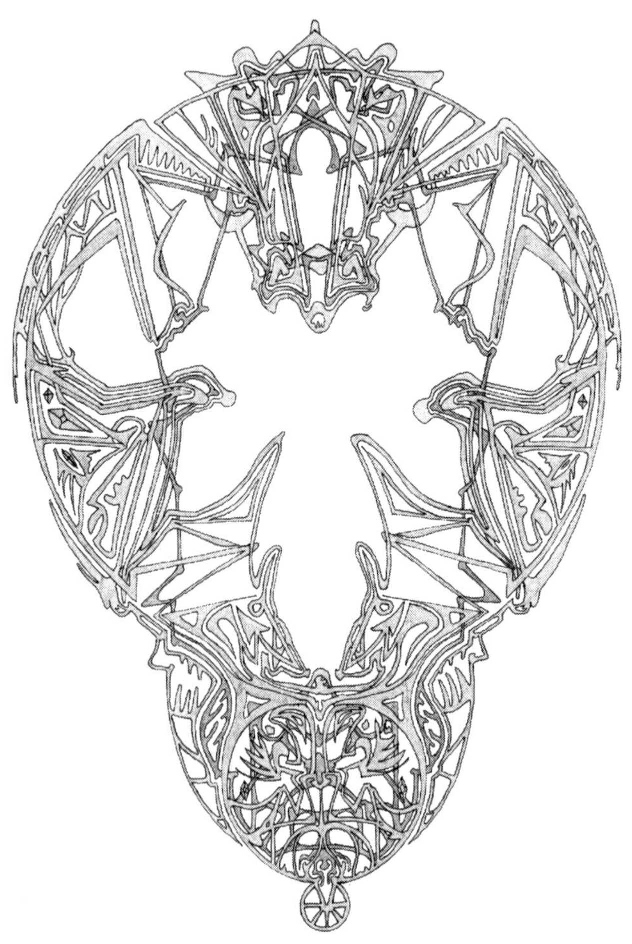

© Sandy Garnett, Armes Mendalla, ink on paper, drawn in rehab.

Day 30 continued Monday, June 19

Dell flipped me for the front seat and I won. The lunatic behind the wheel, a stumpy guy named Sal, drove through heavy traffic at erratic speeds and obsessed over martial arts movies as we careened to the airport.

There was a layover in Dallas for an hour so we smoked butts and checked out beautiful women who weren't tearing their hair out in rehab. We laughed and sulked a bit, looking at the flashing blue neon bar signs that kept buzzing in our brains around every corner; the tipping martini glasses, the mugs with overflowing beers, the drunken patrons stumbling to their gates.

Upon arrival in Phoenix, Dell and I pulled our luggage and were greeted by three sketchy characters. The old one held a sign with our names on it. I started dripping Arizona heat as the two younger guys gave us a harsh introduction to the new lives we will have for the next three months in good old Mesa, Arizona.

"Bart's a hard ass. If you rub him wrong you are fucking out," Tom grinned. Mike agreed with a crooked smile, swaying in the wind, a tall string bean with a large Latin nose and flowing shock of mullet pride. Pops, an old grizzled black man with friendly eyes and white, wiry hair, thin and sweaty in his polyester, took turns readjusting his hat and stroking his meager goatee. Pops was in his own world and I wondered if this wielder of car keys was okay to drive.

Mike and Tom took turns rattling us with house jargon and rules, trying to make us wince. Two young rich pricks on a little vacation, they seemed to be saying.

I wouldn't give them the satisfaction, but Dell started nervously tapping the tassel loafers he'd shined in Dallas. Dell has been playing the white collar New York bachelor for awhile. He's in here for cocaine and booze mainly, which fits the profile.

One of the benefits of moving around a lot was that I became a social chameleon of sorts. I adjusted quickly to changing looks, accents, vocabulary and attitudes in order to blend into my surroundings. Initially, I learned the survivor expression at my grandparents' apartment on 420 East 79th Street in New York City. "Always look like you know where you are going and keep your money in your front pocket," I would hear when I was a little boy on a solo errand in New York City or taking the Tube in London. Over the years I got pretty good at looking like I knew where I was going and what I was doing, even if I was completely lost. The survivor vibe comes in handy when you're chasing your favorite band all over the place, in a shady situation, a hitchhike, a trip to your regional rehab, or a drive through the desert to your local halfway house.

We strolled out in sweltering heat and climbed into the orange piece of shit, wood-paneled station wagon with tires as bald and polished as Dell's head. My game face went on, the emotion drained and I prepared for the worst as we creaked away from the cactus curb, my skin stuck to the torn vinyl seat that was jabbing into my leg.

Dell attempted to relate to our new hoodlum friends with idle Wall Street conversation but he failed to connect. I asked about work. Mike talked about minimum wages unless you have a particular skill, like if you roof houses in 115 degree heat all day. Pops explained that his luxury mobile served as the halfway house cab, so when we get jobs he will take us to work and pick us up for the price of a pack of cigarettes. That amounts to a carton of cigarettes a week if I need a lift. Mom and Dad gave me a check for the first three weeks, and it is expected that I pay my way from then until I get out of this shithole.

After a sullen moment I realized that my luck was not as bad as I was making it out to be on this particular car ride from the airport to my halfway house on an unbearably hot day in the middle of Arizona. It ain't so bad... how do you roll the windows down in this stinking car, though? The wagon flew along and I contemplated the insanity of cruising this Arizona track in a grocery getter full of fuck-ups. The five of us alone would have done some damage, I thought, as body odor and the smell of burning rubber swirled around the back seat of that shit box and into my seething nostrils.

"And don't even bat an eye at the women, or you're out on your ass," Tom warned. Any foul play and we're outski. We are restricted to the grounds for three days to grow accustomed to the system. We will be humbling ourselves by scraping gum off the pavement, picking up cigarette butts, cleaning and sweeping. Mike said that fifteen minutes in this sun is like three hours of sun on an August day in the Northeast, minus the humidity.

We arrived at the halfway house and I pulled my pack out of the car. I was ushered through the kitchen to the back office and presented with forms to fill in, which included a contract to sign regarding Bart's Mesa Halfstep rules. My license was photocopied for the record and I gave the preliminary check to Pam, Bart's wife and the office administrator. Little did I know that the middle-aged black man with a cane who lay sprawled across the office couch was Bart himself. He wore a grizzled, inquisitive expression and matching clothes, his offhanded behavior projecting custodian rather than king. When he asked me what Step I was on in my recovery, I told him that I was on the first Step, just like Tom and Mike had told me to do on the ride from the airport. From what they said, Bart will chew a greenie into pieces if the newcomer tells Bart that he is on any other Step but number one, which is the admittance Step in recovery. Are you working your program? No, I'm working THE Program. Tom and Mike's advice was sound, and with those two quick answers, Bart left me alone enough for me not to realize that he was the real boss until the after dinner meeting.

I went out to the kitchen, which doubles as community space for card playing, meetings, and activities. Josh is here with some of his crew from rehab. I ate a small bowl of revolting stew that was at least filling. Meals are meager I am told.

Here I lie in my new bed in my new apartment with my new fuck-up roommates in a halfway house in the middle of Arizona. I put my things away after the meeting, showered, and now it's time to hit the sack after a long day.

Day 31 Tuesday, June 20

First wake-up at the halfway house. I'm very glad there's air conditioning. Apparently everything here is air conditioned, partially by law I heard.

Last night's meeting was all right. Bart hung around at the podium in the kitchen and spent most of the time ragging on people in the audience. I found his presentation to be harsh but amusing at the same time. One minute he'd be joking and the next minute he'd have one of the residents in tears about something.

He preached that we are all insane and that we will all be on the first Step for a long time because admitting addiction is the hardest thing to overcome.

As Bart says, I don't want to be here, someone persuaded my 'fucking ass'. Now that I am here, though, I might as well get my ass in gear. You have to watch yourself in this place. No one gives a damn about you because soon enough they'll all be gone. Bart screamed repeatedly last night, "YOU IS ALL YOU GOT, MOTHERFUCKERS!"

After the meeting last night I got to my new room in apartment #103. The halfway house is comprised of three two-story units in a row, four apartments to each unit. Each apartment has two bedrooms, two to a bedroom, a kitchenette and a small living room. Everything is drab and cheap - flimsy wood paneling, garage sale furniture, stained carpets, chipped Formica counter tops, a run down bathroom, but the place is clean enough and simple. It ought to be clean as sober people are good at things like cleaning, which is always better than twiddling your thumbs or thinking about old party thoughts.

Two of the apartments have televisions, but as Josh told me, "There ain't no guarantee." I was lucky enough to get into one of the apartments that does have a television because my apartment mates are on 'short time'. Jason, one of my new apartment mates, only has six days to go. He told me last night that he will go back to Nantucket and enjoy the rest of the summer there with his girlfriend. Jackpot Jason.

I unpacked last night, watched some television and went to bed. I slept O.K., nothing special, but I feel rested. Right now it's 7am and 95° outside. People say this temperature is cool and welcome.

Josh said that the three clouds in the sky yesterday were the most he has seen since he arrived in Arizona a couple of weeks ago. There is a small set of weights in Josh's apartment, so we did some minor lifting last night after the meeting. I have to remember to do push-ups, sit-ups and dips every day so I can keep the strength I started building in rehab.

Another compatriot and graduate of my rehab is here also. Goose is a heavy-set brute with chopped blonde hair and a big friendly smile who Ron and I would talk to about working out. I wonder how he's managed to come this far as he is unpredictable and explosive. He told me that the women cat call you in Arizona, they will approach you for conversation's sake, they're beautiful and they have left the East Coast snobbery routine behind. I'm not sure why he was talking about dating propects, as tangos with the opposite sex are grounds for immediate dismissal at the halfway house. Goose gave me two applications for an auto supply store and a veterinarian's office. I could work for a vet. Today I will fill these applications out and do the bullshit jobs Bart's guys assign to me.

This morning, I got to the kitchen five minutes after breakfast is supposed to be over. Allie, the old cook who hollers orders at her assistants while playing an eternal game of hearts and banging down economy cigarettes into an overflowing tin can, let me know harshly that I won't get anything to eat a second past 7:15am after today. I took the news quietly and got out of there as soon as I'd washed my bowl and spoon. We get one small plastic bowl of economy flakes and a crappy cup of instant coffee every morning and that's it.

I spent the next several hours mopping the ratty dining area, picking up cigarette butts and peeling gum off of the sizzling asphalt, then cleaning the utility closet outside with Dell and Goose. I was happy to find some books in the closet that had been abandoned, so I squirreled them away and back to my apartment during a bathroom break.

Lunch here is a one slice bologna sandwich on economy white bread and water or bug juice. We can have mustard or mayo on our one slice bologna sandwich. The mayo is that sweet, cheap stuff I dislike. I was starving at lunch, looking around for leftovers, people who might not want their bologna sandwiches. No luck.

Here I sit in my new temporary apartment on my new temporary chair, looking at the blank screen television. It's dull and boiling hot. We are not allowed to watch television until 5pm, and anyone caught doing so will be put on probation or thrown out on the spot, depending upon Bart's mood. I am restricted from setting foot off of Bart's property for the next three days, so I have plenty of time for heavy reflection. Right now I'm completely bummed out about being here. I guess learning is expensive because it's costing me today. Besides recovery, I'm learning about life one step above the streets.

I am required to earn a living out here. I've always had jobs and I am a hard worker so that's fine with me. I had a paper route when I was eleven, I caddied, watched pets, I cut lawns, shovelled snow, I landscaped in the summers forty hours a week in high school. I worked at an ice cream store, which was great because they had this massive nitrous tank in the back that we used to suck down. The thing was seven feet tall so you had to stand on a stool to get to the valve. What a buzz. You turned the knob on the tank and it blew your hair back, it spat little specs at you while you inhaled, then you'd be out of it for a minute or two. A job that has a massive whippit in the back room to slurp on when you're not eating ice cream? I'll take that one. I delivered prescriptions for a pharmacy, I did odd jobs, and I worked for the town cleaning public property areas one summer. I started selling my art on posters and tee shirts at concerts as well, and bands started to pay me to make art to promote their gigs. This is something I could make a career out of.

Hopefully I can find a job this summer that pays minimum wage. Every cent I make will be necessary to pay the weekly rent and transportation to and from work. I'm starting to wonder if I should even bother calling my parents right now. Maybe I should just write. I miss the luxury of home and family but that's what I had to get away from in order to reassess my values and ideas about life. This place is not a bowl of cherries.

Here I lie in a pool of self-pity. I just got off the phone with Mom. Right now I feel anger and resentment towards anyone else in the world who is enjoying life, because I'm absolutely miserable. When Bart spoke to my parents he told them to give me no more than $10 in cash for the plane ride so I could get some coffee at the airport. I have no money for a soda right now. I have no stamps to mail a letter. I have nothing.

My pessimistic attitude is the first thing I should really try to work on. Is the glass half empty or half full? It's been half empty for the past drunken year anyway. Now that things are beginning to change I have to think of the glass as half full, although my bad attitude twists the truth all around on me.

I have three months to reflect on my life here in Arizona. I should let the leashes in my head go to enlighten myself. This is the real thing, man. I can get only so much emotional support and strength from distant friends and family. It is time for me to depend on myself. By letting go I will give my will up to faith, which can lead my ignorant ass through this trying time. That is the only way I will be able to see the light at the end of this deep and dismal tunnel of hopeless, worthless sorrow.

When I look at the vast world I am reminded of how insignificant I am, how the world does not revolve around me, how the world can function quite well without me.

Given my modest emotional challenges, I might one day realize humility, which seems to be an important component to appreciating the beauty of life, a way of peaceful living. When I look at my luck compared to that of my friends, I may be the one who drew the short straw this time. But when I look at all the unlucky people out there I quickly hone in on what I do have and why I should be grateful for my lot. And you know what? Since I picked this journal up a couple of minutes ago and started writing, I've worked my way out of wallowing self-pity. I feel at peace and I sense a bit of happiness. Suddenly I'm glad I'm here, alive and well with more good luck than most, believe it or not.

I have no place to hide from myself here. I have meager meals to eat and a humble place to live and sleep. I have been stripped of all frivolities, and it is making me frighteningly aware. I have brooded on my lack of physical comfort because I thought it was one of the primary sources of my unhappiness. Looking deeper I realize how this train of thought has the potential to railroad me. Physical comfort, or numbing of the senses for that matter, are distractions that I used and abused to avoid inner reflection. I don't have any type of distraction here. I have the desire to build on my inner self in hopes of ultimately achieving some sense of peace.

My spirits have risen dramatically in the past hour or two. Goose taught me how to play Spades and I spent some time laughing at myself again, which feels good. Humor is one of life's greatest facets and it seems to keep the world spinning in the right direction.

Day 32 Wednesday, June 21

This morning my roommate Jason got in trouble with the staff for virtually no reason at all. The counselor wanted to make Jason squirm. We are woken up at 6:30am and our beds have to be made for the day by 6:45am. We make our beds and sometimes get a couple more minutes of sleep in the living room on the floor or the couch. This dickhead counselor got Jason up off of the living room floor and took him to the office for sleeping late. He was put on restriction after 5pm, which means that after he finishes work he has to come back and spend the rest of the evening in his unit. He said he doesn't give a shit because he's out of here in a matter of days.

Apparently some of the counselors are total assholes and they like to stick it to people. No one likes these disgruntled souls, but what do our opinions matter? Besides, what's the point in fighting the system in this place anyway? Jason told me that there is no use in trying to do things your own way. If I want to get through this I have to do what they tell me and shut up about it. I have no problem with that. If I'm a straight arrow I will piss off those dicks who want to see me fall down.

I've been thinking about what sort of work I could do and what kind of money I could be looking at. There are some likely prospects in the help wanted ads. With a decent appearance and a bit of charm I can get a job and start making some money soon.

Evenings can be relaxing around here. Last night I lifted weights with Josh after the meeting again, then showered and watched a bit of television. My little apartment is pretty cool because this place is like a summer pad away from home. I'll be making my own living and learning about who I really am for the next three months. Not only should I discard my bad attitude and reservations about this place, but I should try to enjoy the experience. Why the hell not? I can read, write, develop my artistic skills, and exercise. What else could I ask for? My outlook today is healthy. I am grateful to be here now.

Day 33 Thursday, June 22

This morning I woke up and hung around with the other residents who are out of work or on temporary restriction. At 9:30am, the older counselor named Ted asked if I wanted to replace this guy Marlo, who got a job through some temp agency. Marlo was poorly dressed for the day of kitchen duties and didn't want the job, so he was asked to find a replacement.

Ted drove me to this big company and picked me up when my shift was over. I spent four hours washing pots, pans and an assortment of gigantic utensils in the industrial kitchen that feeds the building. The work wasn't exactly up my alley, but four hours at minimum wage was welcomed after a month without two pennies to rub together. Ted and I talked about some good things on the way back and I felt like this was a step in the right direction. After dinner, Mark the string bean asked me if I want to take a roofing job tomorrow. Well of course I would, Mark.

Tonight Bart explained that the new program schedule will be implemented this week. "If you don't have a job by Saturday, then you gotta spend your first month going through another rehabilitation situation." In other words, if I don't find something steady by Saturday I will be stuck in meetings all day long for my first month here. Bart's world is too much to handle around the clock, so I resolved to find something fast. I spent the rest of the evening brooding about the new rule, and it really started eating at me. I guess he owns the place and he is the king.

Day 34 Friday June 23

This morning I worked from 6:30am to noon on the blazing roof of a house that was undergoing construction. I loaded and stacked terra cotta tiling for the roofers to lay down. The roof was a frying pan, but I worked hard and did fine. Mark, that pussy, said he felt dizzy and went to sit in the shade of the garage while I carried his load. The foreman dropped us off at lunch and told me that if they needed someone again they would call me because I worked my ass off for them. Mark is out of the roofing business.

I spent the afternoon shuffling around like a headless chicken, burdened by Bart's looming job deadline. I was itching to work, looking for any sort of part-time thing that would get me out of six meetings a day for another month. I asked Bart for permission to go find a job, and surprisingly he gave it to me. This afternoon I found a job forty minutes away at a sports club selling memberships.

So I'm employed now. No more mind power will be wasted grieving over the new system that will go into effect tomorrow because I've found the bypass job in time. I am not stuck here anymore. I begin on

Monday from 6pm to 9pm. I get free use of the gym as well, which is great.

It is not worth fretting over minor complications like work attire or my shift schedule. I spend too much time worrying about things that don't matter. I can't let things 'rent free space in my head' because they distract me from the good I am trying to do. Everything is falling into place.

I spoke with my family tonight. My parents were very happy to hear about the new job and my positive attitude. They will send some dress pants and some shirts that I can wear for work.

My brother told me about a respectable kid from town who was picked up for writing phony checks, draining a buddy's bank account, and stealing stuff to support a drug habit that nobody knew he had. I couldn't believe the news and I'm sorry for his troubles.

I've done well settling in this week. Things are working out because I'm going with the flow, which is one of the hardest things for me to do.

Day 35 Saturday, June 24

Anton is my new roommate, and he snores like a son of a bitch. His driver took him to the wrong airline, so he missed his plane from JFK. He ended up on a later flight and got here at five in the morning. He's a big, amicable enough black kid about my age with scars on his cheek and neck from knife wounds. He grew up in the ghetto and was into everything, but his real thing was crack, like most of the other people here. He talked about getting cracked out and cruising around with his boys. He talked about how some of his friends would go out shooting. They would shoot pigeons, pets and they would randomly shoot at people on occasion. This is what poverty breeds in my country, I thought to myself as I listened to this seemingly nice guy on the other end of the couch, this crackhead from the hood whose friends sometimes used to shoot at people for sport, this new roommate of mine who snores like a son of a bitch. I'll stay on his good side like I do with everyone around this place, keep them laughing, stay out of the crosshairs, not get shot up.

Sarah called Mom yesterday for my new address and they had a good chat. Mom thinks she's sweet and caring, which is a nice endorsement. I want Sarah to send me a picture. I will write her this weekend.

Today we went to the park. Saturday is sometimes park day for the halfway house. We did our Saturday morning chores before we left. You can't slip up or you'll be left behind, restricted or thrown out. Once everyone had cleaned their apartments and done their assigned chores we hopped into the counselors' vehicles and hit the road.

Sitting in the back of an old yellow pickup truck and tipping my cap Arizona style was great. I felt pretty good flying down the dusty roads, passing palm trees and distant mountain ranges on the way. Time for some sun, a little exercise and a hamburger. I hadn't eaten a hamburger in a long time. I busied myself with one-man hacky sack, which was fun and exhausting. For a couple of hours this afternoon we hung out in the public park, a gaggle of addicts chain-smoking in the shade underneath the picnic trees. We got back to the halfway house at 3pm. The roofing guy I worked for last week dropped off my check before dinner. He told me that he can't use Mark anymore but he might call me again next week for some more work. The roofer was sick of Mark's candy ass bullshit by now.

After washing dishes, before the night meeting, Goose decided that this place was no longer for him. Apparently he's about to receive a $1200 tax return, which makes him completely wealthy compared to my presently groveling state. When I went back to my apartment and mentioned that Goose had vented some anger and was now packing his bags, Jason said that he's seen maybe fifty people come and go since he's been here. This was a slap in the face. He also told me that most people are kicked out or give up and get wasted within days of leaving the halfway house. I cannot be one of those people.

During the meeting I caught my first tinge of temptation. I projected myself back at school and I started to worry about braving the party atmosphere. I don't want to drink anymore, but this won't be easy. I've had it with liquor. This halfway house is where my failed efforts have gotten me at the ripe age of nineteen.

I can't expect everything to come to me in the blink of an eye. I am beginning to feel good about myself again. It will be a gradual process, but eventually I will return to college a stronger person. Rehab to a three month halfway house is the first step. The halfway house will make way for a peaceful family autumn as I mend ties with the family, work, and prepare for my spring semester return to school. It just gets better, and tomorrow is another day.

Day 36 Sunday, June 25

The new Phase system began today and it really sucks. We were woken at 6am for meditation group. Welcome to the new Sunday morning program.

This new system that Bart has created on a whim is too much. He has divided the 90 day program into three phases. In the first month a patient is supposed to be restricted to the grounds and must go through more extensive therapy, quantity over quality, six hours a day. The second phase allows us to go find work. When we are not working we are to attend all meetings held at the halfway house. In the third month we are to be sent to one of the units that Bart owns in the next town over, which will mean less rent, more freedom, and no chores or treatment facility atmosphere. I am tempted to tell Bart to fuck off but I'm no fool. I'll rough it out in spite of this fucking asshole. Today we start this new 'rigorous' treatment bullshit program, and people are pissed. I'll just have to observe in silence as other, less pensive members of my new community rock the boat and fall overboard. Tomorrow I begin my new job and I'll be out of here most of the time because I made the cut off day for finding work.

Wow. What a harsh morning. In the past couple hours Bart has made a concerted effort to whip us all with his new program. There has been no organization to this agenda change and the resulting confusion is making Bart angry. He is in the process of weeding out some of the misfits. Tom, the short scraggly one who picked us up from the airport, was kicked to the curb in dramatic fashion. Bart unleashed on Tom and left him on the corner with his bag and an AA book. When Bart throws someone out, everyone knows about it because his screams echo down the string of units that make his little sober kingdom. Bart didn't like Tom's attitude, and a minor incident set Bart off. Tom left with two other guys that Bart let loose on as well. He was screaming for what seemed like hours. He has an impressive street vocabulary. I'm learning that Bart is quite a sight any time he's angry, and since he's usually angry all day long he's always dangerous. I don't ever want to rub him the wrong way.

Goose came back to 'visit' after our meeting tonight. He left on his own accord, which makes him a special case because Bart didn't hate him enough to kick him out, so Goose wasn't told to get lost when he came back to say hello to us tonight. He seems lonely and clueless. His home is back on the East Coast, but out of pride I think he cashed in his tax return and got himself a place around here to prove to his parents that he could still do it, Bart or no Bart. Goose is ruled by his troubled emotions and anger like others here, so I'm afraid it's only a matter of time before he gets himself in trouble again. He rolled in on his new motorcycle and the addicts circled around, all wishing they had their own wheels to blast out of this hellhole.

The saying around here is mind your own business, because minding someone else's will get your ass kicked out. I'll keep my head down and let all the Toms and Gooses trip themselves up without any help from me.

Day 37 Monday, June 26

Jason left us this morning after completing his 90 days. He's going back to Nantucket to spend the remainder of the summer with his girlfriend. I wouldn't mind a little love on the beach of a moonlit evening welcome home present. He's a lucky bastard and I wish him the best.

This morning I ate my usual meager breakfast, a tiny cup of coffee and some econoflakes. I'm starting to get a little hungry these days, but I'll get used to the strict, minimal rations. I cashed my roofing payment check with Bart's wife Pam, who does all the finances. They charge three percent to cash checks. I got a couple of bucks to buy notebook paper, a pen, and cigarettes. I also received a nice letter from Sarah and one from Mom today. Sarah misses me and said in her letter that she will keep writing. This made me feel good so thank you Sarah.

Apparently there was an electrical fire on Friday at the sports club I was supposed to start at today. The girl on the phone told me to call back on Wednesday to arrange another starting time.

I think Bart is going to move a couple of us to Pepper Circle, a second condo concern that Bart imagines as more of a transitional phase to his program. If Bart chooses me it will be a relief to get the hell out of here. But for now, I might as well enjoy everything I have while I've got it.

Here I lie on the floor outside of my temporary bedroom, shielded by the wall from the nosy counselors outside. It's 10pm, which means that it's too late for first phase residents to be awake, according to Bart's crappy new system.

I just finished writing some close friends to let them know what I'm doing out here. I wrote Sarah back yesterday. She's a really good person and her letter of support yesterday helped.

I am doing my own thing and I stay out of everyone's business. It is simple to keep a clear conscience when there is no place for me to hide. I've had a clear conscience ever since I said screw it and started talking honestly, which broke down my emotional barriers back in rehab almost a month ago. Letting it all out of my system has been like draining a wound, but this hard step is necessary in the pursuit of unrelenting honesty, truth and serenity. These are starting to be the most important things in my life, and I'm amazed at how many positive facets of an individual's existence go hand in hand with cleaning the heart and mind. I am learning to appreciate the peace in all of these things.

I just got cut off for a minute because one of the counselors came in to check on us. You have to watch yourself around here. Just play their game, learn to take some punches and you'll make it all right.

Man. Going back home from this place will be a damn luxury, I'll tell you that. There won't be counselors hounding me and pushing my buttons, there will be no curfew, there will be food to eat and a loving family. A drunk can neglect the best things in life. That won't be me anymore. I've got too much going for me, too much to lose and too many 'yets' (I haven't been divorced yet, I haven't lost a job because of drinking yet, and so on). As a sober person I have the world in the palm of my hand.

Day 38 Tuesday, June 27

It took me a while to get to sleep last night. I guess a cup of Monday night meeting coffee and a lot of things in my head made sleep tough. I spent half an hour daydreaming about my old BMW and how gorgeous it could be if I fixed her up. I picked up the 1971 BMW 2002 last year before graduation and my parents were fuming about it. They had always told me if I wanted a car they didn't control that I would have to buy my own. When I drove the BMW into the driveway my father flipped out and confiscated the keys on the spot. I had just been tagged with my first DWI so he was pissed. The station wagon I was allowed to use in high school was the only way my parents could control me when I was not out in it getting a DWI. My father drove my new purchase into the beaten up old shed behind our house, which is where it sits today. I would like to restore the car and make her look like the day she was first driven in 1971.

That car has been sitting on a shelf of dreams and hopes I'm starting to dust off. Today I am curious once again, and this sense of rediscovery is elating and scary at the same time. I feel new and full of life. I have the ability to accomplish goals again now. Goals became impossible last year when I was drinking hard because goals require planning, conviction, dedication. I lost the ability to plan as a drinker because I lived for the moment and never made time for anything that required hard work. I want to shed some light on all of the other goals I put to sleep. I want to know who I really am so I have to keep peeling away the layers. I'm making progress.

Today I went through the fourth step with Ted, who told me I was ready for it. I 'made a searching and fearless inventory of myself', as the fourth step in the AA book reads. The process felt pretty damn good. Ted told me to make a ball of all the anger, guilt, shame and fear inside of me. Once I had done that, Ted took that ball of 'manipulative tools and other shit' I used and 'gave it back to Satan'. He made an imaginary ball and threw it into the sky with outstretched hands and that was that. Ludicrous as it sounds, I felt light and free, relieved at the notion that I no longer have to carry all of that old crap around anymore, thanks to this crazy spiritual witch doctor who is becoming my real friend.

In the meeting tonight I began to play the old "What If" rationalization game with myself, but when I spoke during the meeting it made me feel a lot better and relieved some of the reservations that had built up during the day. I can't challenge the past as I can't change the past. I can only challenge each day as it comes, one day at a time, and accept the results. I can't waste my time brooding about how things could be different if I hadn't gotten in trouble, which weakens my progress and resolve. I must concentrate on how to go about living the best I can today and tomorrow, which settles my mind into a peaceful state. This stuff is all new to me but it has suddenly proven itself to be the most logical and rewarding method of 'being' that I have known.

I've almost been alive for two decades. The older I get, the faster life seems to fly. I can't take this life of mine for granted. Now that I look back, I have regrets about not following through with some of the things I really loved. Today I can work hard and follow through with all of the goals I am starting to set for myself again. I am learning tough lessons at a young age and this is good.

Day 39 Wednesday, June 28

Last night Anton had a nightmare that he'd been shot. I was awoken by the earth shattering lungs of a stranger who happens to be my new roommate. He was screaming, "I'm hit! Go on without me!" I poked him from afar because I didn't want him to wake up swinging. He was sweating and totally freaked out. He cooled off and apologized. No problem Anton.

It's 10am. We've already had two meetings and a meditation. I've got to get working but there is no work again today. The lights in the sports club are on again after the fire, but they are still repairing the air conditioning. I can call early tomorrow to work out a starting time with the secretary. I am trying to take it as it comes.

During the last meeting I expanded on the discussion. I'm only 19 -years-old, I regret the past year of binges, false hope, useless promises and other problems related to my drinking. I've got everything to live for in my new life. I'm stubborn and competitive so I can use these parts of myself in recovery. I'll be damned if anything negative gets in the way. I will grow stronger in spite of people who don't believe in me.

Before freshman year at college I usually achieved my goals, so now I have the ability to achieve the goal I set for myself again. Recovery is my first goal and will remain at the top of my priority list. There are no second chances, because thinking that way is taking back the 'control' element that was my downfall in the first place. The higher power concept is one I've been skeptical of since I heard about it the first day in rehab. I'm happy to be a cultural Christian, a confirmed Episcopalian from early American Protestants, not too religious but with warm memories of church and the nice community of people there when I was growing up. Now that I've been in the trenches for awhile I'm learning that the higher power concept pertains to spirituality first and foremost. The higher power concept follows the 'It's out of my hands' philosophy and is designed to answer questions that have no answers. It can be used to unload emotional burdens that I am tired of bearing. I am learning to let go. I am learning to have faith.

Now that's covered, I'm really starting to miss seeing my favorite band The Grateful Dead. My best friends are about to hit some concerts again. My decisions have left me behind more than once. This is the way it goes.

Tonight I was taken to an outside Cocaine Anonymous meeting by one of the counselors, and it felt nice to change gears with a new setting for once. I was still battling with the past today, so this meeting put me in the right attitude. The past is history and the future's a mystery. I will have 45 days sober tomorrow and I feel good about that.

Day 40 Thursday, June 29

It's Matt's birthday and the family is off for a week to Newport. I didn't get a chance to call because I was chasing after Bart's orders all afternoon. I hope he has a nice birthday.

Bart's lodging system seems to be based on pushing peoples' buttons. You don't get too comfortable with your room or apartment because you have to pack up and move to another unit in a moment's notice. The staff suddenly rounded everyone up this morning and told us to move all personal effects from apartment 104 to apartment 203. The residents of apartment 104 returned from work and tried not to lose their shit, although were visibly very pissed off. I don't agree with this whole thing but I kept my mouth shut and did what I was told. This is Bart's place, he makes sport of messing with us every day and if I don't do exactly as he says I'm out of here. I start work tomorrow and I don't want any trouble. Today is my forty-fifth day sober. Nice.

Day 41 Friday, June 30

This morning I got a message from the office to call home. The office has the only phone in the place, aside from the grungy pay phone outside under the dingy fluorescent lamp where the addicts line up to talk to their loved ones at night, chain-smoking, guzzling soda, crying, pleading, screaming, apologizing into the receiver.

I called back and wished Matt a happy birthday. He is getting that computer he has always dreamed of. He's chipping in on it, which shouldn't deplete his self-made fortune. My brother has always made money and saved it, whereas I've always made money and spent it on partying or art projects for concerts as fast as humanly possible. Matt told me that he set up the fish tank and it's looking great. Fish tanks are funny things. You get inspired, you set up the tank, you buy the fish. Eventually the tank tips over, the heater blows up and electrocutes the fish, or they starve because you forget there are fish in the stinking green water you haven't changed in four months. The fish die, you notice, the tank goes into the closet for a year, until that intangible spark of inspiration compels you to do it all over again.

Mom and I briefly discussed college. I told her that I understood her reservations about my return to the same school. I look forward to the day when my mother trusts me and believes in me again. I lost the privilege of trust in my family and it tortures me. I know that rebuilding trust will take time, but my mother's apprehension hurts. I got off the phone frustrated and saddened.

In the Narcotics Anonymous meeting tonight I spaced out and thought about my eventual return home. How will it be? I flipped through the Big Book (AA book) and was uplifted by Bill's story, one of the founders of AA. Wow, that guy was a train wreck for twenty-five years. When I leave here I will have to use the tools I've acquired as a weapon in order to defeat the dangers of temptation, this looming thing that creeps around in the shadows of my mind.

Today Pops gave me a ride to work and I walked in at 11:45am. Upon entering I could tell that I was screwed. "Oh sorry, the generators haven't been put back on yet. Weren't you supposed to call?" So my first day was canceled. The secretary told me that I can start tomorrow at noon.

I left frustrated and steaming in the pants and shirt I'd worn for work that my mother had sent me. I had a change of clothes as I had planned to work out after my shift was over. I didn't want to go straight back to the halfway house because meetings would take up the rest of the day and I was sick of that bullshit, so I went behind the sports club, changed into my shorts and tee shirt next to the stinking dumpster, then I found some meager shade under the strip of canvas awning that lined the small plaza. I took a seat on the smoking hot pavement, pulled out my book of the week, my water bottle, and I spent the next several hours reading. After finishing the book and water I trudged to the burger joint across the way and gorged on fast food for the first time since I was admitted. The trolley and the bus rides back to the halfway house were time consuming but pleasant as I inhaled the hot air of freedom. Today I feel a sense of direction. I finally got a foot in the door at a job that can be steady.

Dell and I talked about my return to college. Whatever happens, I just can't pick up a drink. It's really that simple, no excuses. Once I am secure with that notion, I can do whatever I like because I don't get in trouble when I don't drink. I asked Dell how many of his college party buddies had settled down. He scoffed and told me that he couldn't really think of any.

My clearing noggin can actually process thoughts in a human, logical way again. My brain is starting to race these days now that my body and mind are no longer numb and inactive. This new head is fun and has its benefits as well as its aches and pains. I've always had a knack for extremes. Now I am on a purity kick, the first positive extreme I've been on in some time.

It gets very dull listening to people talk about the same old preachy, processed, prepackaged AA language, so it is refreshing when a meeting is strong. Usually there are a couple of people in each meeting with interesting thoughts. I shared in a self-mocking way how recovery has taught me that when I was drunk my life was full of rationalizations, minimizations, justifications, how normal I thought it was to go as close to the edge as possible, how my life had started to slip. I put life on hold each night, and those nights had turned into weeks, which had turned into months. I was slowly destroying all aspects of myself. In recovery I am learning this lifestyle was not normal and would never bring me peace or happiness.

Denise got booted tonight. Mark, the string bean, was right when he said that people get thrown out of here all the time. Six people have been thrown out by Bart since I arrived. The bastard has a trigger finger so you have to watch your ass and stay on his good side, although I don't think he has a good side. Apparently Denise's mother had a nervous breakdown and her family is in complete shambles. Denise has been freaking out lately, so Bart pulled the plug on her. That's some placid scene she'll be going back to. Well, I wish her the best of luck, but in all honesty, I'll give the girl a week before she hits the smack again. Bart says every night in his meeting, "The people who fuck up around here get left behind, so don't look back after them." That's the name of Bart's recovery game, take it or leave it. I guess that's the name of the game in life, Bart or no Bart.

Day 42 Saturday, July 1

A lot went down today. Right now I'm at Pepper Circle, the new location that Bart wants to turn into the transitional phase of his treatment program.

This morning, after an extensive cleanup of the halfway house, I was ordered to get all of my stuff, including the bed I've been sleeping on, and told to put it all in the back of Ted's old yellow, rusty little pickup truck. I hate dragging beds around without another set of hands to help.

"We're moving out!" hollered Ted to the small band of us that Bart had chosen to test out the new transitional phase of his program at Pepper Circle. I sighed to myself, knowing that this would mean I would be late for work. It was 10am and Bart's labor assignments usually last an entire morning or afternoon. If Bart tells you to do something, time becomes obsolete. Work? Fuck you, boy. As pissed as I started to get, there was really no sense in getting frustrated. What does getting frantic do for me when things are out of my hands? With this settling thought I just went with the flow, which I'm beginning to realize is much better than fighting.

The Pepper Circle "townhouses," as Bart generously refers to his newly acquired units, are admittedly nicer than the halfway house apartments. The identical two-floor, two bedroom units have a sliding glass door and a back door also, which is useful. The unit that I moved into does not have air conditioning until tomorrow, but even this life threatening deficiency is worth the new address. The eight of us are staying in the unit that has air conditioning tonight.

The move didn't put too much of a dent into my work, but trying to figure out how to get to my job from a completely new location was a different story. I ended up taking a bus going the wrong way for half an hour after following the advice of Drew, that nitwit. Finally I arrived at work after a couple bus transfers and trolley stops. I changed in the bathroom of the fast food place again. The people at the booth nearest the bathroom looked at me oddly when I passed by them in completely different attire, and the young boy pointed at me in recognition of my costume change.

I read while I waited for an hour in the reception area of the gym, taking note of the pretty girls who walked by. The owner, a short, mean little weasel named John, went over the material with me before I began. I sat at the phone from 1pm to 5pm with a phone book and a sales pitch sheet, which I was required to lay on anyone who was unfortunate enough to field my call. The guy across from me, this pencil dick with a buzz cut, a sales smile that looked like a used car, wearing a crisp blue button-down with a couple of pens sticking out of his shirt pocket, gave me pointers on how to bring a live one into the boat. I appreciated the tips but I still found it hard to bait people into a sale by hammering the absolute necessity of a gym membership into their skulls. Mrs. Johnson, look at your waistline with all due respect! You need this program for your future health and happiness. Besides, we're offering you our lowest membership fee ever.

I found one victim, lots of answering machines, a couple of quick hang ups, and several abusive people who swore and told me never to call their house again. One guy said he was coming down to kick my ass.

The experience was degrading, kind of like living with a bunch of fuck-ups in rehab or this halfway house, for example. I got nothing all day, but the seasoned veteran across from me hooked three or four people, which made me wonder if I sucked at this job or this job just sucked. Buzzcut told me not to worry, that I'd get it quickly. His sympathetic offerings made me feel no better. I don't like being reassured by a pro that within a week I'll be as good as he is.

After my sum zero shift I discussed full time employment with the secretary. She said it will take me a week or two to get the lay of the land and learn the packages and programs. This job is supposed to lead me into training people, something I would be good at and enjoy. Yeah, yeah, just get me off the phone and put me on the floor already. I reserved that thought, thanked her and left for the day.

At the fast food shack I bought a soda so the manager wouldn't have me arrested for changing clothes in his bathroom again. I called Nance, who acts as secretary for Bart, and she said that she would send Pops. I hate waiting to be picked up. I feel like a sixth grader again, calling my parents after one of those Walter Schalk Dance School classes when I was twelve and too bashful to ask a girl to dance with me.

I sat on the edge of the plaza sidewalk feeling like a bucket of sweat and trying to get into the new book I picked up yesterday. While I waited for my ride a couple of beer-swilling cheese balls pulled up and one of them asked me for a cigarette. "You wanna swap for a beer?" he asked. That's all I needed to hear. I found humor in their kick-ass set-up, a 1978 jumbo red pinstriped pickup, fully loaded with the gun rack option, huge tires, fog lights, a massive grill, and a stereo that blared outdated disco from a bygone era. I gave the guy a cigarette and said no thanks to the beer. He laughed when I turned down 'an ice cold one' on the way back to the truck and his friend joined in. I felt like a loser for a minute. The truck revved up and peeled away from the lot and its passengers let out a "YEEHAW" in unison as the clouds rose up and enveloped me in waves of enthusiasm until I was caked. "This ain't my day," I said out loud, choking on their dust.

It was a relief to get back to some understanding addicts who know a thing or two about the type of guys I had just encountered. Talk about ridiculous circumstances and overwhelming temptation. The sun was beating down on a 115 degree scorching afternoon, the heat unbearable and depressing. Then, out of nowhere, a shotgun oasis drove by and asked if I wanted one of the ice cold beers that were swimming around in the cooler. "You had to find me," I thought to myself. But I stood my ground, and in doing so I said no to a drink for the first time to an outsider. "Gee, sorry, but I'm a recovering drunk so can I take a rain check on the cold one Mr. Redneck?" Look who's calling who a redneck. My neck is redder than that guy's today.

Thankfully the cook had set aside two slices of halfway house pizza for me. I vultured dinner and washed it down with several cups of that wretched bug juice. It's the first time I have enjoyed one of the marginal meals the halfway house has had to offer. As much as I found the meal satisfactory due to complete starvation, I chased the crappy sugar shot of bug juice with water. This comes from a guy who polished a brick of microwaved Mad Dog 20/20 in five minutes and routinely banged down three shot Vodka hogs with warm beer can chasers last year.

After dinner we got in the car and were shuttled to our new home at Pepper Circle. I said good-byes to a couple of people on my way out the door. I will probably see them again but nothing is for certain here. I've gotten used to spending days in and days out with a heavy rotation of characters. I've gotten to know who smells and who doesn't, who's funny and who's not, who's going to get the boot and who's going to make it. The bond breaking of the daily routine is refreshing as much as it's like leaving something behind. "I'll see you at the meeting, Jim, I'll really miss your stinking feet, your crappy jokes and your obnoxious laugh." There is a certain sentimentality attached to even the simplest of partings because we sit around working through heavy personal stuff together in meetings all the time, and you never know when someone is going to get the boot, so there's always an air of gravity between people in recovery.

Ralph arrived today, and I got a chance to welcome him before I headed back to Pepper Circle. Ralph was in my Group Therapy sessions back at rehab, so we've gotten to know each other pretty well. He's one of my young adult peers, and he was tagged for trying to get involved with one of the ladies back at rehab. His mind always seems to be on the women, and as much as I can appreciate the desire to seek female companionship, I wonder if it will hurt him out here. Knowing Ralph, he'll get caught up in a romantic soap opera with some girl and Bart will kick his ass out. We'll see what happens, but I strongly doubt that he'll be able to think with the head on his shoulders while he's here. Ralph will have a tough time making it through this place in one piece, but that's not my problem. He's a good guy and he's almost as funny as Randy was in rehab, so I wish him the best.

My temper has tested me all day and I spoke with Dell about that. Dell reassured me that looking back just screws you up. He reiterated the concept that when you look back, the good times always seem to outweigh the bad. That's been my problem, because anytime I look back I only see the good times and the fun I'm missing. My mind plays those games on me all the time, and it's a tough game to fight. Dell's words settled me down a little bit.

I experienced the lowlife behavior of an outsider today and it was tough. This drunk guy was waving a beer in my face and asking me if I wanted one. Today I came to the realization that I'm not ready to live in the world of outsiders and I feel much better in a structured program. Maybe tomorrow, but not today.

We got back to Pepper Circle and I played Spades with some of the guys before a meeting was called to order. The eight of us will soon turn into twelve of us, according to Bart, because Bart owns another unit next to these two. In order to get into a semi-structured routine we will have to run our own nightly meetings. I was glad to start up a meeting as I really needed one to get my mind off of the garbage I had gone through today.

Halfway through the meeting that the eight of us had started, Ted came in and stole the show for a while. He talked about serenity, then surprised us by taking us all out for coffee. Crescent Diner was full of people who had just gotten out of AA meetings around town. Ted told us that this was one of the spots that a lot of groups come to after their meetings, which I found cool and interesting. It felt good to hang out and relax, although at the same time I was inhaling industrial strength coffee at an alarming rate without noticing it myself. One of my rehab buddies asked if I was looking to stay awake and alert for three days, and the table laughed the joke off. I'm not laughing about it anymore though. Everyone has long since fallen asleep, and I dread the waking hours as I write. It's about 3am and I'll be up at 6am.

It's good to get out from under the noses of the KGB back at the halfway house. Bart's staff is unbending and relentless, always breathing down our necks and leaving us gasping for air. Room checks occur almost daily, apartment inspections for cleanliness every other day. The sign-in and sign-out board is monitored and can be used as heavy ammunition by a pissed off staff member. Before you leave the halfway house, you have to sign out on the board. Neglecting to do so can result in a week's restriction, which revokes every privilege you have at the halfway house, including the morning cup of coffee. And if Bart's in a nasty mood, he'll kick the most minor rule breaker out of his halfway house. The whole thing is pretty hectic so it's good to be away from all the constraints and rules. Bart has decided that the eight of us are capable of living in a transitional way, where those elementary rules and hounding staff members are no longer in our faces every minute. I welcome the change.

It's time to get some sleep. Tomorrow should be relaxing around here. I'm exhausted, but the massive doses of caffeine I whaled down at that restaurant still have my head spinning. I'm not used to so much diner coffee and so many good laughs.

Day 43 Sunday, July 2

Mark the string bean has recently been promoted to the rank of junior staff member, which unfortunately gives him the right to make us squirm in any way he sees fit. What a shithead. He really fucked with me today.

Bart told Pops, the halfway house "chauffeur", to drive Mark over to Pepper Circle at 5am to kick our asses out of bed. I assume that Mark was pissed off because Bart had gotten Mark up so early, so he woke us up with a vengeance. He walked into our unit, screaming and hollering and smashing his favorite intimidation stick on the furniture. We were all roused, but in a period of five minutes he came around three times and yanked the pillows from under our heads. I slept on the floor last night so Mark stepped on me and started nudging me with those cheesy high tops of his.

Mark is obviously not used to his position as a patient-basher yet. He felt the need to establish himself in an aggressive display that went way beyond his usual asshole demeanor. We cleaned up our sleeping areas, mocking him, swearing quietly. As I was folding my sheets he burst in again and screamed our chores out at us a third time. I whispered to myself, "I know what I've got to do." Mark heard this and approached me with anger. "It looks like you're copping a big attitude, mister. I think you deserve a write-up, and I don't think Bart will like it too much." He slammed the door and I started sweating.

Write-ups are a big deal at the halfway house. Since Bart and his staff are a bunch of short fuses with small pricks, the simplest slip can lead to instant expulsion. I had done a good job at staying the hell away from any trouble until now. When a staff member or Bart is pissed, you have to keep your mouth shut and take the punches. This morning I slipped and I started dreading the consequences. If I get thrown out of here my family might just toss in the towel, whether or not I stay sober. The court will have my ass also as they are expecting my clean bill of health from this place.

I shaved and dressed by 6am but Mark decided that I was being too slow and started breathing down my neck again. I took the heat and went outside to sweep the asphalt in front of the units as Mark had demanded. Sweeping asphalt accomplishes nothing, but the job sucks and is time consuming, so staff members dole out that punishment or task all the time. I made the asphalt as clean as you can make asphalt. Mark came out to inspect the drive and gave me more crap. "What about this butt and this butt. You missed these cigarette butts. You didn't do what I told you, and Bart will be furious." I tried to level with him. "Come on, Mark. You ordered me to clean the drive, and I did what you told me to do. I'm trying to work with you, and you keep giving me shit. Why do you want to shaft me so badly today?" Mark ignored my plea and walked back inside, shaking his head.

The other guys had gone to the store, so I was left to wallow in anger until a ride came. Nathan pulled up and I got in the back of the truck while Mark took shotgun. I jostled around in the bed of the truck with the wind blowing in my ear, hanging on for dear life while Nathan took hairpin corners at fifty miles an hour, watching through the rear window of the cab as Mark talked to Nathan. When we came to a stop light, Nathan rolled down his window and yelled back to me, "You got some problem with Mark?" I gritted my teeth and responded, "No Nathan, I've got no problem with Mark." I wanted to kill that fucking asshole.

When a staff member has a problem with a resident, soon it is apparent that all of the staff members dislike the resident. And once you're targeted, usually it's just a matter of time before you're sitting on your luggage at the corner of Bart's property with your AA book in your lap and your thumb in your mouth, waiting for a taxi to the airport. Nathan is another one of Bart's henchmen, a thirty-five year old who became a staff member a couple of weeks before I got to Arizona. As my ass bounced around in the bed of the truck on the dawning streets of Mesa, I didn't like the outlook of my run-in with Mark. If Bart was pissed, I knew I'd be in danger.

Once we got back to the halfway house, I frantically awaited Ted's arrival while Mark and Nathan went into the staff room off of the community area. Bart hadn't pulled in for the day yet. Ted's the old hand here, and he's taken a liking to me. When he drove in, I went to his truck and talked to him about the pickle I had gotten myself into with Mark. After hearing my story, Ted told me in a subtle way that Mark had been a little out of line because he's not used to his new authority yet. Ted also reassured me that I would not get written up if I sat down with Bart and talked about the whole thing calmly.

Bart finally got in, and after Ted had a chat with him, Bart called in Nathan, Mike, and me. Mark gave his weak and ineffective story, and then I respectfully gave mine. Bart was in a decent mood today, and I think that he hates me less than some of the other people around here. I was grateful when Bart offered that the whole situation had been a simple misunderstanding between us. He told us to shake hands and get along from now on. I think it's funny that any time staff goes too far it's a misunderstanding but if it's my fault I'm out on my fucking ear.

As I was walking out the door Bart told the staff members that they would have to find an in-house cook for the twelve of us who will be living at Pepper Circle and I spontaneously exclaimed, "I'll be the cook, Bart! I've been cooking for two years!" I really pulled that one out of my ass, but I'm starving for work, paychecks and more food. I don't know why but Bart nodded his head and agreed that I could be the Pepper Circle cook.

It wasn't until I got out of Bart's office that I realized how lucky I had been. In the course of a conflict I had resolved a pressing problem and struck gold in the same blow. The cook job means that I live rent free and I get to stuff my face all I want. I can really make out like a bandit on this deal. I can still swing the sports club part time. Breakfast is econoflakes and shitty coffee, lunch is bologna and bread every day with no sides, so I just have to cook dinner for twelve every night. No problem!

Today was beautiful. I've been at peace with myself since I resolved the morning's crisis. In the afternoon we cleaned up all three units with Bart's free labor staff and tomorrow I will move into my unit because the air conditioner should be working by then. Everything just fell into place today, which happens when you go with the flow, according to Ted.

And now I've got it all on paper. Everyone can press any buttons they like, but I'll weather the storm and write a book about it to let recovering people see how I dealt with tough binds like this one. I laugh at that dimwit who sits in the corner wondering why everyone here hates his guts. It's important for me to avoid any future conflicts in this place at all costs.

Here I lie on the floor in one of the units at Pepper Circle. I got word today that two of my best friends, Ken and Walter, will be at some concerts this week along with 100,000 other fans. As much as I'd love to be there with them, I know it's best for me to be here now. I will have time for fun if I prove to myself that I can make it in here. My family is in Newport for the 4th of July week and I hope they are enjoying themselves. I wish everyone the best. I really mean it because I'm no longer envious. I'm happy right here today.

Day 44 Monday, July 3

I'm getting used to tough days as a sober person. Before I got into recovery, if I was frustrated or pissed my anger would give me the incentive to get blackout drunk that night. These days I don't need a drink in order to deal with my problems. Actually, drinking is the last thing on my mind today.

So much happens in so little time around here. Yesterday Bart gave me the cooking job, which got me all high on myself about free rent and an extra $100 a week at the sports club the way I set it up in my mind. Well, things didn't work out the way I wanted them to, as usual. These are the pitfalls of planning results.

Some of my new unit mates, Danny, Josh and Chuck spent Sunday afternoon away from Pepper Circle while a couple of us worked on the new units for ten hours. I prepared the kitchen for cooking amongst other odd jobs all day. Chuck pulled into camp early evening just in time for our self-run meeting at Pepper Circle. By that time the word had gotten to Bart that three of his new transitional residents had been out all day, running around town like they owned the place while they blew off their chores. So during our meeting, Bart walked in, flanked by Nathan and Ted. Bart teed off on us about Josh and Danny. Apparently those dickheads were still watching a movie in town. Bart continued to yell at us and called us a bunch of fuck-ups and misfits, then told us all to get the fuck out and wait in the driveway so he could talk to Ted and Nathan alone. The six of us went out into the still Arizona night and cursed Josh and Danny for causing this problem. A couple of minutes later, Bart stormed out of the door and hopped in his Cadillac with Nathan. As Bart's big black Caddie peeled away, Ted told us that the Pepper Circle transitional phase would never work and we would be moving back to the halfway house. I lost my cooking job before I had cooked my first meal.

This morning I was up at 6am and stacking all of the mattresses in the back of Ted's truck again. We made a couple of trips, returning all of the things to the halfway house that we had taken to Pepper Circle several days ago. I'm sick and tired of being a one man mobile unit, but they use me because I take orders, I shut up, and Ted has helped me. Pick up all your belongings and put them there. Now take all your stuff and move it back here because I just changed my mind! I fight to stay numb about it and not analyze these ludicrous exercises.

Here I sit on my backpack on the pavement of the driveway at the halfway house. The move back was hectic, and as I sweat my face off in this dismal heat, I hope that I might be moving back into the room I left when I went to Pepper Circle. It's almost time for me to take a couple of hours of buses and trolleys to work, and OH SHIT! Josh is out of here! There goes Josh, racing down the stretch, running like a clucking bird with a cigarette dangling out of his mouth! Close on his tail is Bart, waving his cane and yelling obscenities! YOU'RE OUTTA HERE, JOSH! That guy deserves to get booted after the crap he pulled at Pepper Circle, skipping out on us to see a movie and look for girls in town while we worked all day and had a meeting. I wonder when Danny's going to get thrown out. He's the next target I think. One false move and he'll be history too.

I spent two hours on and between buses getting to work. I cold called from 1pm to 5pm but did not find a prospect. Nobody was interested, nobody would hear me rave about the tremendous importance of a lifetime gym pass, that we take all major credit cards and our discounted rate was impossible to pass up. But I worked hard and I really zeroed in on the sneaky things gym membership phone solicitors have to do in order to hook potential clients. I didn't rope anyone but I was feeling sly and devious. I was getting to feel comfortable with the bullshit I was telling my potential customers. Some of them actually stayed on the line, which gave me a chance to lay my new routine on thick. I was beginning to get it.

When my shift was over I checked out with the secretary. That complete asshole John, the sleazy little club pimp, took me aside and began to address my sales incompetence. "Due to your lack of phone solicitation skills, you will work on a commission basis until you prove yourself." I paraphrase as his English was so bad. The silver chain that rested in a bed of matted chest hair protruding from his blue v-neck polyester workout suit caught one of the ceiling strobes and blinded me as I pleaded with the fucking prick. He didn't care that I had spent nine hours of work time in his shitty establishment, and he didn't listen when I told him that I'd spent the same amount of time commuting to and from his sweat shop. I felt like ripping the rug off his head, ramming it down his throat and kicking his teeth in but I didn't. I walked out of his place without throwing a piece of workout equipment through one of the twelve foot tall windows and without a red cent for my efforts.

Today I learned that phone solicitation is not for me. I also realized that I don't want a sales job that requires me to wheel and deal. I'm trying to abandon the bullshit, so why should I have a job that demands the slippery tongue that got me here to begin with? I am trying to leave the art of manipulation behind me, so I need another line of work.

It was good to get back to the halfway house after a

long day. I ate my slop gratefully and headed back to my new unit, which is not the one I moved out of before going to Pepper Circle over the weekend. I was exhausted, tired of the fight involved in forcing things that don't want to happen. I tried to let go of the frustrations today on the way home, which helped a lot.

Nathan just came in and told me that I will be moving again. An hour ago I finished unpacking, and now I have to move it all once more. I've been dragged through the mud for days now. I've been hired, fired, screamed at, and I have moved too many times to count. I'm beaten down and I need to recharge the batteries.

Day 45 Tuesday, July 4

This morning I moved my belongings into apartment number 206 this time. Today we get to relax because it's the 4th of July so I will reflect on my progress. I've come a long way in the past several months, and it's nice to be aware of that. I lost clear self-awareness in the haze of booze for a year but now I am learning to look inside myself again. Maybe on the other side of this experience is manhood.

Day 46 Wednesday, July 5

Yesterday I flipped the frisbee around with Dell before we left for the public pool. It's funny how the smallest things are significant these days. I would have laughed before at the notion of going to a public pool, although I went to public pools in New York City when I stayed with my grandparents growing up. A lot of my friends have a pool, or they belong to a club. Now I see life from another angle. My ego is obliterated in order to make way for humility, gratitude, new vision, a yellow public pool.

The whole lot of us went to the pool and I sat in the water all day. I swam around casually like a lazy turtle, enjoying the feeling of being out of the sun but in it at the same time. Thirty recovering drug fiends frolicking in a public pool, happy as pigs in a pen. I ventured to the diving boards, one of my favorite spots as a club rat. I used to get to the club during those pre-high school summers at the crack of dawn with Matt. I would run around with a tennis racket glued to my hand, a towel draped over my shoulder, a soaking wet prune from the pool, eyes stinging from chlorine, hair bleached in summer sun, a popsicle sticking out of my mouth on occasion. That's how I spent two or three summers of my life when we came back from England and they weren't so bad.

I pulled a marginal one and a half off the low dive. When I started high school I didn't have time for diving boards as I worked summer jobs. It's a good thing to be young. There is no reason to try to be older than you are, which all young kids seem to do when they are growing up. People spend their first 25 years wanting to be older and the rest of life trying to be younger. Maybe I can be happy with my present age and leave it at that.

We got back to the halfway house and had one of those things that Bart refers to as a picnic, with Hamburger Helper and all. I read and played a third game of chess with Scott, one of my new apartment mates. He gave me a chess book and I skipped through that for a while. We played four games by day's end and drew two games to two. Chess is my favorite game.

I remember when my father took a bad fall on an ice patch in the parking lot of Pittsburgh International when I was seven-years-old. He got up off the ice and hobbled through the terminal. He didn't want to miss his return flight but he probably figured that a broken ankle in Pittsburgh was an acceptable excuse. I was the one who picked up the phone to hear him babbling in a drugged out stupor that his ankle had been broken in three places, it was bad, they would have to cut him and that he would like to talk to Mom please. My mother got on the phone and tried very hard to contain her amusement as her wasted husband lay there with a shattered ankle trying to speak incoherently through a wicked morphine buzz, falling in and out of consciousness during the conversation. My mother kept trying to wake him up by screaming into the receiver. "Alex! Are you still there? Wake up!"

My father returned from the hospital three days later with a cast that went up to his knee. He spent six weeks camping out in the den, driving my mother up a wall. He grew a beard, read the paper, bent a couple dozen coat hangers to scratch his itching leg, which my mother confiscated as a lancing might lead to gangrene. We must have played two hundred games of backgammon during this time, and he won ninety percent of those games. He kept a record on a yellow legal pad that sat to the left of his chair next to an ash tray and the Winstons he gave up on his 42nd birthday after my grandfather died of lung cancer. Dad taught me chess while killing me at it, which is what college team chess players do to their eager-to-learn sons. Over the years I got better and actually beat him once in high school, but those games faded as our relationship splintered. When I go back home I think I'll brush off the old chess board. I look forward to seeing that spark of excitement in my father's eyes that reminds me I am proud to be his son.

Today I finished my fourth book in six weeks. That's

no major accomplishment but this new reading kick is a start. By the time I leave Arizona my goal is to have read sixteen books, or a book a week. That would be decent.

I received a nice letter from Sarah. She was happy to hear that I am doing well. I'm not strapping anyone down so I hope she realizes that she has to come first in her life too. I wrote letters to Sarah, Ben and Wayne today. Ben and Wayne are two of my best friends from college. Ben already knows my situation and I wonder if he filled Wayne in.

Tomorrow I will look for another job in my town instead of two towns over. I'm doing well and I am trying to keep my head up.

Day 47 Thursday, July 6

Last night I couldn't sleep much as I projected into an unknown future. I've got two plus months to go before I return home to my family. I woke up thinking about the transportation issue, the legal issue, I wonder about my old BMW and if I can repair that, I wonder about work, where my life is going.

It's easy to get wound up. I've got to keep in mind that none of this should worry me. I'm heading in the right direction, which is all that counts now. Today I've got to concentrate on getting a job so I can pay my rent, which is starting to stress me out.

I think about going back to school. If all goes well I should be full of direction by the time spring semester rolls around. I have trouble realizing how pathetically blind I was last year at college. My job is to study and grow there, to take advantage of the experience and make myself a better young man. Something down the line stopped me dead in my tracks. I have taken this opportunity to reflect on my past and change what I can about myself this summer. I will get a chance to live at home and mend ties with my family for a couple of months before I return to school.

I woke up feeling shaky after a tough night but I have managed to alter my morning perspective and my gratitude returns.

Day 49 Saturday, July 8

Yesterday I was pissed off about the lack of jobs out there, so I spent the morning brooding. The new rule that Bart put into play on Thursday night is that no First Phase people can use the phone. I'm riding the line between the first Phase and the second Phase because I have had a job and I was about to become part of the Pepper Circle transitional Phase, all of which fell through.

I wondered if Bart would throw me out the window if I used his pay phone, so I asked for permission to set up some interviews. Bart got all pissed off and made me feel and look like an asshole. "Are you in Phase 2?", he asked. I don't know, Bart. "Then why do you think you get different treatment? Are you God's gift to this motherfucking earth? Get the fuck out of my sight!" So I went back to my room and sulked, writing an 'I want sympathy' letter to my parents. I had to explain in detail to them why their poor son couldn't call them and ask them how their great trip to Newport was.

At dinner I was still chafed so when Ted strolled in I explained my frustration to him. Ted lit a cigarette and piped up, "Why didn't you slip out and use the fucking phone at the gas mart, you stupid asshole! All along you've been breaking Phase I rules with Bart's unspoken consent because he thought you could handle work, the kitchen job, the sign-out privileges. Don't cry on my shoulder, you peckerhead!" He told me that when I asked Bart to use the phone in front of everyone I spoiled my own good thing. He explained that Bart already has enough assholes on his hands so when I have a problem I should talk to Ted about it.

Later in the evening Ted spoke to Bart, who grudgingly agreed that I could begin the second Phase on Monday. Sure enough, Ted was right on the mark again. I have to drop my bad attitude and chill the hell out.

Today I spent the afternoon with Ted over at Pepper Circle cleaning the units out, doing whatever I was told to do, free labor, yammering away with Ted, absorbing his stories, his philosophy, his good energy.

During dinner, back at the Mesa Halfstep, it rained for the first time since I've been here. The rain was short and hard but it felt good to stand in for a couple of minutes as it cooled off the Arizona heat. Everyone was ecstatic about the brief change in weather. After the rain, steam coated the pavement and rose from the trees and the cars. I stood in the parking lot for a street sauna and watched the sky as the rain disappeared.

When I come to this journal I find that I can often write myself out of a terrible mood, this familiar face that listens but does not judge me like everyone else around me. I will start writing in anger but I end up writing through the anger and into some sort of happiness. This journal provides relief.

I don't know exactly what was going through my head earlier today. My mind is always playing tricks on me in recovery, and if I don't keep an eye on it I fall into what I like to call a 'Rationalization Episode.' These episodes can occur at any moment during the day and are difficult to keep under control. One moment I'll be singing the sweet song of life, then suddenly I find myself pissed off and wishing I wasn't here. I start thinking things like, "If I hadn't gotten in trouble I wouldn't be in the middle of Arizona at this flea-bitten halfway house," and then my mind starts racing. Rationalizing kicks my ass like Bart talks about all the time. He stands at his podium whacking that cane to the rhythm of his consonants, yelling, "You're all fucked up! You're all insane! And if you could all have your own fucking ways right now, you'd be six feet under in no time!" I end up beating the hell out of myself and it hurts. I just have to keep my mind in the present because I can't change the past. I have to accept my life as it is and go with the flow.

Earlier today I was thinking about good times and how the hell I can still have them with my old friends if I stay sober. I started getting scared, and emotionally speaking, I started to reach out for a drink to take the edge off of an imagined social situation. Is that not the most fucked up thing? I don't want to drop my friends for the sake of recovery, and I am afraid of losing them. In rehab and here at the halfway house, they are always hammering it into our skulls that we can never go back to our old friends because old friends lead to old habits. I don't know how much I agree with that, though. If I am going to hang out with my best friends when I go back home, I have to be strong and learn how to socialize as a sober individual. If a situation freaks me out I just have to remove myself from it.

It will take some getting used to in order for me to feel comfortable in these arguably dangerous environments. I have plenty of time before I have to deal with that, so it shouldn't even be on the daily itinerary right now. Where does 'beat yourself up' fit into my schedule?

This journal is good. It has become an excellent outlet and relief valve, and I've gotten a lot of writing out in the past few months. I have written myself into a reflective and peaceful state again.

Day 50 Sunday, July 9

I just wrote to the Dean of Student Affairs at my school to let her know that I will be taking a leave of absence in the fall. I'm glad that's finally out of the way, because it's been in the back of my mind for a month. Last night during the meeting I spaced out while Bart's screaming echoed in the background. I've been away for almost two months, and I can hardly believe the ways I've changed.

It feels like only yesterday that I was skimping bong hits and smoking cigarette butts out of the ashtray every hungover morning at school. What did I get out of my first year at college? I learned party endurance tactics, administrative bullshitting techniques, how to scrape by without going to classes, where to put my jacket so I wouldn't lose it when I blacked out. I learned how to slow down my chemical and alcohol ingestion just enough not to pass out, I learned that I couldn't make a 9:40 class, I learned that I couldn't make a 10:50 class, I learned that without a couple of drinks in my system I had become a social retard. What else did I learn? How to suck down a four shot hog without puking, how to shoot caps, how to get a speeding ticket at 7am, how to drain sludge from the fraternity basement, how to weasel in the music I wanted to listen to at a party, how to con others into saying O.K., how to put my hair in a ponytail, how to run on ice, how to fall on ice, how to cut off my own cast, how to dance on a torn ankle at 4 in the morning to get a cast in the first place, how to use crutches, how to hide my feelings, how to kiss ass to elders, how to minimize the smell of weed that seeped out into the hall and got passers-by suspicious or stoned, how to borrow class notes politely, how to ignore term papers and class assignments, how to walk into class late, how to fold a futon, how to urinate on a futon, how to convince my parents that I was really excelling, how to make fake ID'S, how to scam for freebies whenever possible, how to arrange my music effectively, how to pad my trash can spit bucket with paper lining, how to make a giant Vodka bottle collection, how to slip in and out of dull or exciting scenes, how to tap kegs and pour the best beer, how to minimize my problems, how to amuse or horrify my peers, how to set and snooze an alarm clock, how to break an alarm clock, how to get a second DWI, how to get packed off to rehab and Arizona.

Day 51 Monday, July 10

A packet of letters arrived that my Mom forwarded to me. My college friend Iraine sent me a black beaded bracelet that I put on before writing her back today. When I receive a letter it cheers me up and is good for my morale.

I just got out of the 7pm meeting. Bart's oration technique and messages are very effective and make me think. Man. When I look back at all the crazy shit that I pulled in the past couple of years, I really can't believe it. How many drunken nights did I crawl to the car and make it home? I would close one of my eyes and try valiantly to stay on the yellow line. How many times did I wake up in unfamiliar settings and not know whether I had even driven the night before? How many times was I embarrassed because I had to admit that I didn't remember meeting someone who told me that we had spent an hour chatting the night before? How many times did I black out? How many times did I pass out? Look at the places I passed out in; cars, woods, bathrooms, parking lots, beaches, country clubs, hotels, boats. How many classes did I miss because I was dead to the world? How many alarm clocks did I throw out the window? How many injuries did I sustain in drunken stupors? How many DWI's did I get? How many times did I lie? How many times did I make promises? How many times did I break promises? How much did I procrastinate? How much did I minimize, rationalize, justify this behavior? How much of my life have I already thrown down the toilet?

Today these things make me sick to my stomach. No one in his right mind should have to ask questions like this about himself. I was insane, clueless, a true lost soul. I'm very lucky to realize these things today at such a young and promising age. I'm tired of it all. I want peace, happiness, and everything that goes along with leading a decent, hard working, normal life. I want my family back too, most of all. My party animal image has died and can go into the Hall of Fame for Fuck-Ups. It took a lot of diligent self-destruction to achieve such a distinquished award. Now I can move on to bigger and better things. I chose the wrong path at the right time I guess. I can't imagine choosing this path as a middle-aged divorcee with kids, work, a home and a ton of expenses. I do what I have to do and keep moving down the right path. I'm one of the first of my generation at the height of this rehab craze. Eventually a lot of people in my age bracket are going to find out that they need to change course. They say it just gets harder to change the longer you stay on an unhealthy path.

Me? I don't need a drink today because a drink represents insanity, death and relapse in my life. I don't want it anymore. I'm a lot happier today than I ever was when my lips were stuck to the bottle. I don't need to take crap any longer either. Today some moron came here from my rehab and drank himself into a blackout on the plane. He arrived totally wasted and tried to tell me that he'd only had a couple before Bart threw his ass off the property. I told the guy that he was an asshole and that I wasn't taking any of his shit today. Stay the hell away from me!

Day 52 Tuesday, July 11

Same old morning routine. I read and hung around for awhile after the meeting until lunch. Being on the grounds with the new Phase system means that I have to attend numerous daily meetings that are held by counselors and staff, and that is like rehashing rehab all over again, although it's not as well organized. I can't wait to find steady work so I can get out of here every day and make some money.

After lunch I ventured down to the gas mart, a short trek through a deserted lot, overgrown by Southwestern vegetation and tumbleweed. Dell told me to watch out for venomous snakes. "Did you know that in the state of Arizona, more people die of snake bites per year than babies drown by falling into unsupervised pools?" What an awful statistic. I kept my eye out for rattlesnakes and scorpions as I made my way through the empty lot. Maybe I ought to stick to the sidewalks.

I tried unsuccessfully to arrange some interviews at the gas mart pay phones. I slurped feverishly on a slushie as I tried to make out the phone numbers for job leads that I'd scribbled onto a piece of paper. Some construction worker was on the other line and all pissed off that I was invading his personal space with these two public phones glued together in the parking lot. I guess I was spoiling the intimate atmosphere he was trying to achieve with a loved one as he burned through cigarettes and whispered into the receiver from a public pay phone outside of a damned gas station. People are territorial about the strangest things.

Aggravated and on the verge of heat exhaustion I called home and reached Matt. He told me his trip to Newport with the family was a nice interlude during an otherwise hectic summer. Matt relishes family vacations, eating well, sleeping long and enjoying the good things that parents sometimes bestow upon their vacationing kids. In the past several years I avoided the annual family vacation. I was too busy rebelling to appreciate the family getaway concept that my brother so easily accepts and enjoys. "Sure, Mom, I'll wear the shirt you bought for me, I'll go with you on a sight-seeing adventure, I'll eat the restaurant meals, I'll play board games with the family, and I'll be nice to my little brother before Christian hits the hay." Why couldn't I see this simply in the past couple of years?

Matt took my father to his second Dead concert. He said that Dad was proud to be wearing one of the shirts I had silkscreened. He brought along some friends from his office, and I had fun visualizing the scenario. I can see Dad sitting on his buddy's tailgate, shooting the shit with wandering hipsters that populate the parking lot carnival before the concert. Matt said that Dad was cool, that he liked to get a glimpse of where his oldest son has spent months of his life. Matt's the kind of accommodating soul who will cater to Dad's enthusiasm at being included. I was embarrassed by my parents so I would never include them. Maybe this is one of the things I can change about myself. I need to appreciate the enthusiasm of my loved ones instead of being embarrassed or intimidated by their excitement, which might just mean that they love me. It is good to be loved.

Matt talked about how the household is like a pressure cooker and how he is starting to take a lot of the heat that I used to take. Since I'm no longer an outlet he is beginning to feel more of that tension. Mom and Dad have to concentrate on their own stuff in order for the family to become healthy as a unit, but they are also trying to raise three sons and this is harder than anything I've ever done. Mom has spent an eternity of sleepless nights worrying about her kids and this is part of the parenting deal. They have taken the first step by being open and supporting me, so they have to continue on that path. When I get home I have to focus on my own path. They can try to take on my problems and blame me for things but that won't be my ax to grind any longer. My family will have to learn to accept that I have changed. I will no longer be the family scapegoat so I won't take the guilt if I'm doing my job as a healthy family member.

Day 53 Wednesday, July 12

This morning I spent my last two bucks making useless phone calls for interviews and a one-way bus ride downtown for a fruitless job hunt. I am broke again and without a job, so this minor problem has turned into a nightmare I can't seem to shake. I don't have a penny to my name but I am expected to come up with rent money for Bart next week.

Nathan, one of the staff members, told me that he has seen me searching hard for work, that my conviction to find work warrants a bit of help from my parents. He said that if I really need some money for rent or to continue searching for a job I shouldn't kill myself about it. He will ask if Bart needs any extra paid help. I like Nathan. He kept me from beating myself into the ground today.

Day 54 Thursday, July 13

Today I began to address manhood and how it differs from youth, according to Ted. Ted took me out all day with Bruce and Tammy, two other people who have worked hard and are searching frantically for a job. Bruce and I hopped into the flatbed of Ted's old yellow pickup truck and we drove downtown. Ted dropped us off at the corner. He told us to walk down Main Street and apply to every single store on the strip, which spans several miles. Then Ted and Tammy were off as we stood in their cloud of dust.

I have learned not to question Ted, who has proven to me that method does exist in madness. I have spent hours talking to the man, who has taken an interest in knocking some sense into me. His philosophy is so simple. I am learning from a master.

Bruce and I split up the street, as walking in together to apply for a job didn't work too well. Store owners and managers were reluctant in general, mostly because they all had a pile of applications and no work. We walked down Main Street for three hours and submitted applications to as many stores as we could. I kept Ted's simple thoughts of going with the flow on a loop in my head the whole way.

Noon came and so did the lunchtime AA meeting spot at the end of Main Street that Ted had told us to go to when we had completed our task. The meeting proceeded and we listened to a bunch of sympathy groveling as people moaned about their financial difficulties in recovery. Sometimes meetings turn into gripe sessions so by the end of the hour I couldn't wait to get out of there.

Ted picked us up outside and we drove over to see a stone statue of Jesus, which stands tall in the atrium of a Mesa church. Then we went to the town hall where he showed us some Mesa history. I didn't know what Ted was getting at but we just kept hopping in the truck and going where Ted took us. The next stop was the Village Inn, which is Ted's favorite diner for lunch. He gave the waitress a dollar when she seated us. He told us that he gives waiters and waitresses a buck when he is seated so they treat him well and tend to him first. I couldn't believe my ears when he told us to order whatever we wanted for lunch, that he would treat the three of us. I ordered a grilled cheese with bacon and fries, which was completely delicious after three weeks of the halfway house menu.

A couple weeks ago I discovered that Ted knew how to fix up old cars, and since then I've been bugging him about car restoration. During lunch I asked him about fixing up my BMW again. He took a long look at me through his coke bottle glasses, he pulled some coins from his pocket and instructed me to call Brand's Reconstruction and Repair, which was listed in the Yellow Pages dangling by the pay phone that he pointed at. I asked if I could finish my meal and he told me that it wasn't going to gallop off anywhere, that I should call first then finish lunch.

We drank a bunch of coffee while smoking a lot of cigarettes, the two remaining vices that recovering addicts cling stubbornly to. By the time we left the Village Inn Ted had found job opportunities for all of us. We got in the little yellow truck and were off, flying down the palm tree-lined roads of Mesa.

We arrived at Brand's, which took forever to get

to, out in the desert behind McDonnell Douglas Helicopter Systems. Bruce and Tammy stayed in the truck as I followed Ted into the small, dusty office. He introduced me to Clem, who owns and runs the body shop. The quiet bearded giant stood stoically in a grease stained orange shop suit with his name tag sewn askew on the chest, wiping grime off his big meat hook hands to shake mine. Ted told me to look around the place while they talked.

On the way to the body shop, Ted had screamed out the rear pickup truck window that he had taught Clem a lot of what he knew about fixing cars. The bond was clear when I saw their eyes meet. I started poking around the shop, trying to imagine how anyone could have taught such a wise man like Clem, who looked like he had been born with a blowtorch in his hand.

The garage fit three cars and a ton of tools, and there was an adjacent storage garage that fit two cars on deck. I was intimidated but excited by the gutted cars and car parts that littered the floor. While Ted and Clem spoke I found the wall of before and after photos from old cars that Clem had made beautiful again. I started thinking about my BMW when Ted and Clem came in and interrupted my daydream. "You see that '73 Ford?" Ted pointed at the wall of pictures. "Well Clem and I cleaned up that fucker in two days for an old friend. Remember that one, Clem? He'd bent the piss out of that axle, and we come along and told him we'd straighten the fucking thing right out. No one believed us, but we sure as hell managed. The body all fixed up a week later, and she looked fresh out of the fucking box she came in!" Clem nodded steadily, his hands mashed nervously into his pocket, his modest face attempting to conceal pride. As Ted and I were leaving I told Clem that I would call to see if he could use my help. I wondered if I would soon join this group of stern, hard working men as I bumped around like a sack of potatoes in the back of the pickup truck. The wind started howling and we were fast again in the Mesa heat.

On the way back into town we stopped at Ted's trailer home, where he lives with his wife of thirty-five years. I made a collect call to Mom and Dad upon Ted's instruction. Ted got on the phone with them to explain my new job and how I would need a week of rent until I got my first check. They had no problem with that, but when Ted handed the phone back to me Dad asked nervously if I was now thinking of making auto body work my future full-time occupation.

We finally got back to the halfway house and I spent some time in Ted's office talking about the day and my new job. When I asked about getting a ride to work, Ted belted, "That's your own problem, you fuckin' asshole! You want me to hold your pecker when you take a piss too? I got you a job today, you shithead. Now make something out of the gift you've been given, or to hell with you! Go on. Get the fuck out of here before I beat you with the fucking Yellow Pages!" he screamed, motioning towards the three-inch phone book. Ted screams a lot. It's his way of telling me that he cares.

I called Clem before dinner and we agreed that I would start work tomorrow at 8am. The body shop is in the middle of the desert, probably ten or eleven miles away. The walk will take me two and a half hours each way, so I'll have to leave the halfway house tomorrow morning at 5:30am to make work on time. I'll work hard, I'll walk home and I'll have something to tell my parents about tomorrow. Maybe they'll lend me some money so I can get a second-hand bicycle, which would reduce my commute significantly. I know from what Ted tells me that Clem and I are compatible and he will take me on if I bust my ass for him. Today has been a blessing. Wake up at 5am.

Day 55 Friday, July 14

Last night I peeled the label off of an empty plastic two liter soda bottle, filled it with water and put it in the kitchen freezer. I made lunch, a one slice baloney sandwich between two pieces of economy bread, my twenty-fifth bologna sandwich since I arrived in Mesa. I'm not a fan of bologna really, it's okay, but I'm starving at lunch so I'm happy to eat it. I woke up at 5am, showered, I put the frozen water bottle and the sandwich bag in my cloth backpack and set off at 5:35 am.

The walk took me two hours and twenty minutes. The desert highway heat got close to 100 degrees. The two liter bottle of frozen water in my cloth backpack thawed completely by the time I arrived at the body shop, just before 8am. I drank half of the water on the walk. The sandwich took the shape of the water bottle and became a soggy river. I figured it would dry out in the fridge at work a little before I ate it for lunch.

Clem brought his five-year-old son Ryan to work today. Ryan taught me how to change the sandpaper on the orbital sander. I spent the morning sanding one side of a blue 1972 Plymouth Barracuda. At lunch I sat in the concrete shade outside to eat my sandwich and swill my water. Clem told me to watch out for scorpions if I was sitting down near car parts, which scorpions hide in. Twenty minutes later I was back at work, sanding down some doors and a car hood. I finished the day by cleaning up and performing a few random tasks that Clem asked me to do. The walk home was long and hot but peaceful. I filled the water bottle up again, which got very hot against my shoulder blades as I walked the highway through the blazing sun. My mind wandered as I walked. I thought about home, school, what I want to do with my life, the art I want to make.

I got back to the halfway house with a dirt tan from sanding all day and from walking through the dusty desert swirls while sweat poured out of me. When I walked in Bart pointed and laughed at me, then he started screaming at me to clean up before entering the common area so dirty. "Get the fuck out of my kitchen and shower your ass up before you walk on in here you asshole! You look like a motherfucking raccoon!" I did look like a raccoon as I had my sunglasses on all day long around my eyes, which were the only parts of my body that were not caked in sandpaper dust or desert dirt.

I showered, ate some slop and called my parents. I asked if they would help me get a used bicycle but my parents didn't really believe that I had walked five hours to and from work today. I know what I did and I'll do it again every day next week. I'm off for the weekend.

Day 56 Saturday, July 15

A resident named Jose left while everyone was asleep. If you're going to leave this place, you might as well do it like Jose because Bart isn't there to humiliate the hell out of you in front of everyone while he's kicking your sorry ass out the fucking door, as he puts it. Even Jose's closest friend here had no idea that he was going to leave. He said good night as usual, he had his bags packed, he slipped off into the evening, off into the shadows, off into the rest of his life. He is weak so my guess is that he may be wasted again already. The thought of sitting on my luggage at the curb of Bart's property is a complete nightmare and cannot happen to me.

This morning we cleaned our apartments, as usual, and then I went down to watch half of the "Bill's Story" movie. Bill is one of the founders of AA and one of the writers of the AA Book. I have trouble imagining the thought of spending twenty-five years of my life as a hopeless drunk. My little stretch was plenty.

I've had several drunk dreams lately, waking in a cold sweat, horrified that I had picked up a drink again, only to realize that it was just a bad dream. I am coming up on 60 days sober and I wouldn't give that back for anything.

I haven't gotten mail in a week but I don't need to rely on concerned friends and relatives for positive reinforcement to tell me that I'm doing well right now. I recognize that when sober I can accomplish anything, whereas when I was a drunk I could not even climb a flight of stairs. I miss my family. My parents know that I am changing for the better.

Afternoon. I just learned another important lesson from Ted, who is rapidly becoming my mentor and tough ass guiding light. He called me an asshole and said that when I'm given an inch I take a mile. Last night, after Mom and Dad considered my request for the funding of a used bicycle, Ted let me know that I had already been given a lot of gifts so I have to use the tools I have been given and I don't need more enablement. So what did I do? Today I called my parents and told them that I would work the bicycle out myself.

I got off the phone and Ted called me on my bullshit. He said that I force everything to my desires. "To want what you want when you want it is the biggest addict hang up of all, you asshole!" Ted screamed. He asked me what my primary concern was today, and I reluctantly admitted that getting a bicycle for Monday was more on my mind than anything else. He said, "Exactly. That's how you force shit. You can't put a bike before the program."

I told Ted that I'm impatient and I always want things now. Ted told me that I have to let that go. He said that to hold onto desires like that is forcing life, which results in dashed expectations and is dangerous. "Last night you asked your parents to help you get a used bicycle, then you called them back today and told them you need to do that yourself. You left your loved ones confused in the middle of your bullshit. Stop being such a fucking asshole!" Ted yelled as he lit another cheap cigarette, kicked the ground with his cowboy boot, got in his yellow pickup truck and peeled out of the driveway, leaving a cloud of Mesa dust as I stood there sputtering in its swirl.

Day 57 Sunday, July 16

This morning I started thinking about stupid old stuff again. A meeting snapped me out of it. My priorities have really begun to ingrain themselves. I am relearning how to live honestly. I'm not battling with myself as much anymore. I have no guilt or shame today. I have to stay in the now and I will grow stronger.

Day 59 Tuesday, July 18

During the meeting tonight, while Bart was busy screaming about how we're all stupid motherfuckers, Pops pulled into the parking lot with someone he had just picked up from the airport.

This kid walked through the door in mid-Bart scream, wearing a hat and a nice collared shirt, with his golf clubs over his left shoulder and golf shoes in his right hand. I pulled my hat down over my eyes as Bart's eyes widened. Our new resident said cheerfully, "Hello, my name is William, and I'm an alcoholic and addict! Where do I check in?" The room lit up with laughter like a Christmas tree. William laughed along at first, then he started to get nervous while Pops brought in two more pieces of luggage. I have never seen Bart speechless, but he really did pause for a minute. 'What the fuck am I gonna do with this insane country club motherfucker?' he seemed to be asking himself. Pam came out and quickly escorted William back to the office, almost as if to protect him from the onslaught that hung in the air. I will never forget Bart's face when he stopped screaming, turned to his left to see the new guy, all chipper and smiling, standing there with his golf clubs in the middle of thirty chain-smoking, pissed off drug addicts.

Day 61 Thursday, July 20

The week has gone well. With the help of my feet and thumb on one occasion I have gotten to work on time every day. I've done a lot of sanding and I have become acquainted with some of the tools in Clem's shop that blanket the walls and drawers of the garage like the Mesa dust.

Clem is a good man. Yesterday he offered to give me

a ride home if I helped him move some things out of storage. After work I climbed into the back of his pickup and we drove to his storage shed. I helped Clem for an hour, moving greasy, heavy machinery onto the bed of his big truck. Ryan contributed his five-year-old strength, very focused on making himself useful. Ryan has been at work with us since I started last week. On the way back to the halfway house we stopped at Clem's home, which has a big backyard full of car parts. His wife and children came streaming out of the front door and Clem swept a couple of his kids up with the slightest of ease, kissed them, and then told them in a loving but firm voice that they should stay back while we unloaded an engine block.

Today is my thirty day mark here at the halfway house. Tomorrow I will get my thirty day chip, which is a tactile symbol of accomplishment. Before I flew West they gave me a metal coin that reads, "Day by Day". Sometimes I carry it along, flipping it as I walk through the scalding desert to that old garage behind McDonnell Douglas.

Life has been good to me since I have finally begun to respect it. When I was drinking I had so many expectations of myself and other people that I was never satisfied. Today I concentrate on the present and I don't have expectations, so good things that come along become great surprises in life. This is not a bad way to live.

I almost forgot to mention a dream I had last night. I was speaking to the first man on the moon, Neil Armstrong, and he talked about what the future holds for man in space. He told me that there will be three spacecraft, each the size of a football field, assembled in space and inhabited by humans. He said that one of the crafts will be stationed on the moon and the two remaining crafts will orbit the earth. I find the dream notable because of some news I heard on the radio at work. The disc jockey announced that today was the anniversary of the first man on the moon, and he talked about a moon base and a spacecraft that are being created right now, each of which is estimated to be about the size of a football field. I never heard or read about this before until my dream last night.

Day 62 Friday, July 21

It's been a week of hard work, and now I can relax and enjoy the first weekend I've really earned in over a year.

I've been learning tools, methods of body work, and how to most effectively support Clem in the shop. This morning I accepted Clem's suggestion that he pay me a dollar under minimum wage per hour for the first couple weeks of work. I was hoping for double that but I'm not complaining. My paycheck for six days is a whopping sum compared to the past several months of having no cash at all. Ted told me that he has a bicycle to sell if I want it. It needs a little work but it will do the job.

I can't imagine how great it will be to have my own transportation again. I walked 23 hours through the desert to and from work this week. Walking is rough on the feet and mind but I got used to it and there is a cleansing element to it. I listen to the sound of my walking figure as my mind drifts and I think about what I want to do in life. With a bicycle my commute will be cut way down.

Day 63 Saturday, July 22

I'm learning to take all of the good things in mind and be thankful. I used to brood over insignificant mishaps in my free time but I'm not doing that anymore. There's no point in remaining captive in the past as life moves on and never stops for anyone.

Ted and I went to Pepper Circle, where some of the old hats are living now, people who have done their 90 days and are transitioning out of Mesa as soon as it works for them. We walked in and I started talking to the guys but Ted wasted no time. He went out of the side door and returned with an old, beaten up silver ten speed. As Ted wheeled it out the front door, without saying goodbye to Scott or Jim, Scott said feebly, "That sucks. I was gonna fix that bike up." Ted disregarded Scott's lame objection and we left him to sulk and play more cards with his roommates. I threw the bike in the back of Ted's truck and we were off. Ted started to do a funny imitation of Scott being a candy ass, whining about a bike that was not his to begin with while he did nothing but play cards and smoke cigarettes in the kitchen all weekend.

We went by one of those check cashing clubs, which infest every row of stores around here. NO I.D. NECESSARY! WE'LL CASH ANYTHING! The cashier informed me that in order to cash a third party check I would have to become an honorary member of the club. Honorary my ass. They took a photo, a membership fee and a hefty percentage but I really didn't care because for the first time in months I had a pocket full of money after a week of work, a feeling I remembered as I always worked through high school when I was not doing sports.

I paid Ted fifty bucks for his bike and spent a couple more bucks at the bicycle shop. Ted dropped me back off at the halfway house, and after two slices of Saturday Night Special pizza I went to work on my new bicycle. I replaced the inner tubes, hand grips, I added a water bottle and attached a cheap air pump to the frame. Mike the Bostonian helped me with the brakes and handlebar adjustment, and after realigning the wheels I was good to go.

The evening meeting ended and I decided to give my bike a try. Bruce also has a bicycle, which is a rare commodity here. Bruce by the way did not walk through the desert for a week to get his brand new shiny bike. We signed out and rode down to one of the local restaurants to sit for a burger. I felt like a rich man. A couple of guys stumbled in and we quietly ragged on them for having a hard time keeping straight faces while they tried to talk to the cashier about their takeout order. "Look at those waste products. They're going nowhere fast." On the ride back I felt the power and freedom of having my new transportation. The bicycle rides like a dream. The air was warm, sweet, and the lights sifted by as we zipped through the crystal streets back to Planet Bart.

Good things are happening to me after several difficult months of hard work. The saying goes that it only gets better, and I have trouble picturing life better than this. I can't ever remember feeling so content as I do at the end of this day before lights out.

Day 64 Sunday, July 23

Bruce and I ventured off to the public pool today. I gave the bike a decent workout and it can take some abuse, so it will be good to me this summer. I reacquainted myself with the high dive like I'm getting to know a bicycle again. I haven't stepped outside without my shades since I arrived in Arizona so I tried to tan the raccoon eyes. I polished another book off and we returned for dinner.

Mom said I am working hard and starting to shine again. I love her very much and I appreciate the attentiveness of my parents these days. It's a new feeling to speak openly and be heard all the time.

A new resident produced another chess board so there are now two chess boards floating around. I beat Jim and Paul earlier tonight. I love chess for its strategy, for the people and conversations it attracts, and the way chess exercises my strengthening mind.

I have to remain humble and active so I can continue to grow and get better. I have a bicycle for work tomorrow and I look forward to giving it a run on the desert highway.

Day 66 Tuesday, July 25

The desert is nice on a bicycle. This thing is a slow, old beater, but I love her and she puts a huge dent in my round trip to and from Brand's every day.

I have been prepping a 1957 Ford Fairlane 500 Skyliner power retractable hardtop, which made waves when it came out way back then. The roof comes off on hinges and folds itself into the trunk, which I find fascinating. I've busted my ass sanding and priming that car since I started work and we finally got ready to paint it tonight. One of the four old cars in Clem's shop is finally going to see the light of day again. I'm learning a lot at the body shop and the bike makes my life a lot easier.

Day 67 Wednesday, July 26

I finally got up the nerve to ask what happened to Clem's pinky. The tip of his left pinky is flattened like a cartoon finger that has been hit with a hammer. Clem was sitting at his desk, eating lunch as I looked at his wall of restored car and truck photos. He told me that he used to transport houses. He pointed to a large photo on his wall of pictures and there he sat, driving a massive vehicle with a house on the back. One day when they were unloading their cargo a house fell on his pinky. It was an entire house that squashed his pinky finger. He said they lifted the house back up and the last part of his pinky was flattened like a pancake. He flipped his cartoon pinky finger around and mentioned that he was surprised it had not popped right off. I lost my appetite and went back to work.

Day 68 Thursday, July 27

I've established a pattern of arriving at the shop on time, working hard and learning what Clem teaches me as quickly as I can. Clem and I get along well. I think he likes having a good listener around, although he doesn't talk much. Today I made a little house out of sticks where the garage door opens. Ryan started to get into the game, imagining that nuts, bolts, sticks and rocks were cars and people. Clem saw him playing with the new formation of sticks and rocks from his office. He walked out to Ryan, kicked over the formation and gave his son a hammer. I pretended not to notice and kept my head down, sanding away.

The bicycle ride to work is pretty easy and has gotten quicker. I'm beginning to develop some stamina and learn the most effective ways of approaching the various asphalts and roads I travel on to get to the shop. I've had the chance to spot some interesting desert dwellers. I've seen road runners, snakes, jack rabbits sprinting across the range, a number of bird species, some large wolf spiders and a bunch of lizards, which run cheap in Arizona pet stores. This morning I saw a scrounging coyote as I rode close to the last turnoff of the low-slung industrial park in the middle of nowhere I commute to every day.

The scenery is gorgeous around the work side of town, which is really just desert. The fringes of Mesa prove to be outstanding viewpoints to watch the sun rise at dawn. The mountains are sprawled like carpet in the backdrop of every sideways glance. Clouds hang lightly and lazily over the jagged, flowing ranges on the horizon. The pillow clouds gather and cast rainbow colors from the sky around the large land masses in the distance. It's quite a sight, riding to work every morning. It would be nice to take pictures but I don't have a camera, so these images have to embed themselves in my mind.

I've been away ten weeks and here in Mesa almost six weeks. Things are moving fast now. I suppose time can move fast with some peace of mind. I've worked hard and the insights I've gained have been remarkable. I have been at a serious self-analysis camp between college semesters.

My brother told me awhile back about a kid in my town who just got pinched for stealing money from the bank accounts of relatives and friends to supplement his drug habit. I have been thinking about his situation.

He was on his way to college this fall, a good student who was active in the community. This kid's in deep trouble, facing some heavy charges. Unfortunately for him, the whole town knows. My grand finale of a second DWI looks like peanuts in comparison. No one really knew what happened to me. Summer began and I didn't come back. I just walked out the back door and got into treatment without a big stink. Sure, there are a couple of know-it-alls in town who check the police blotter first every week but this is not so widespread. Drinking is the accepted form of self-destruction in our culture and includes the evening scotch swillers who look at local police blotters. Cocaine, theft, and perjury don't go over as well as a story about a stupid kid who gets a DWI. Does that make my load lighter? I don't know, but that kid back in my town is bumming his ass off right now.

I miss my family and I will be happy to see them when the time comes.

Day 69 Friday, July 28

I got back from work to hear that Ted went to the hospital today because of chest pains. I was shocked to hear the news, but oddly enough I continued on with my after work routine. Now I feel guilty because I care about this cowboy oil man who has given me so much insight. I told Tammy I will go with her to visit Ted as I miss him already. I don't know why, but the thought of Ted's dying struck me hard tonight. I really hope he will be okay because he means a lot to me.

My thoughts are with you Ted.

Day 70 Saturday, July 29

Today I received a picture of Sarah that I asked her to send. She's a pretty, attentive, intelligent, warm person. I showed the picture to my halfway house buddies. They all think she's beautiful. I felt proud to hear that from them, not just because I have a pretty girlfriend, but because she cares.

I got back early from the 'banquet' that Bart spontaneously decided to throw for everyone, which meant some ice cream and a bit of dancing in the kitchen. The rap music cranked and all I could think about was being home or at a concert with my friends, so during the party I began to isolate and defocus. It's easy to tell when one of your halfway house friends is thinking about old baggage. If I'm not happy people smell it right away. I came back to my unit and thought about my friends, school, Sarah, my future, and how Ted is doing.

My thoughts are with you Ted.

Day 71 Sunday, July 30

I had a great conversation with Mom and Dad this morning. We talked about Ted and how I would like to visit him in the next couple days. Ted's a tiger, I told my parents. He'll be all right. We talked about if my old college is the school for me to return to after all this. My parents have really been brooding about that question and I mentioned that it is still six months away. I told them that I've already come so far, and that I'm not going to do something like go back to school unless I'm prepared. My college holds a strong support system of friends for me, which can work to my benefit if I'm careful.

Mom voiced her concern about the lack of alcohol counseling at college. I will need meetings, not alcohol counseling. I've been counseled enough, and meetings are the medicine once I get on the outside again. My father noted that this was a very good point. My parents told me that they are very proud and overwhelmed by my progress. My father said that today I speak honestly and with a strong sense of peace. I've changed so much.

Day 73 Tuesday, August 1

Yesterday I was sanding a car door at work when Ryan, who usually bounces around harmlessly, became alarmed out of the corner of my eye and ran into his Dad's office. Clem emerged, grabbed a shovel and walked over to a fender that lay against the wall next to the garage door. He peeled back the car part and kicked a black object into the driveway. I followed Clem out into the asphalt sun with Ryan. The thing started to move but Clem wouldn't have any of that. He took the blade of the shovel and diced it like a tomato, over and over again. Ryan got close and Clem told him to back off as he scooped the thing up and tossed it towards the low brush next to the dumpster. "Scorpion," Clem said as he walked by me, shepherding his son back into the shade of the garage.

Day 75 Thursday, August 3

Ted returned after five days of recovering from his 'mild' stroke. In most cases, a stroke victim is out of action for weeks, months, or life, but Ted isn't in the 'most cases' category. The man chews iron and spits nails. It's a relief to have him around again. He's walking slowly but he's not doing the Frankenstein as there was no paralysis, so he can still hold his coffee mug in one hand and chain-smoke with the other at the same time.

I'm starting to move up in the world of auto restoration. I am taking pride in the work I do at the body shop as my knowledge and experience deepen. I get to the job on time, I bust my ass and go home satisfied every day.

I feel very accomplished and have good reason to be in this hard earned frame of mind. Forty-five days at the halfway house. I've reached the halfway mark and I feel the changes. I've come a long way in the past few months. I've learned a lot about life. I'm beginning to like myself, something I lost last year when I was drinking.

Day 77 Saturday, August 5

On the way back from the gas mart this evening I saw several police officers questioning a driver they had just pulled over. I returned from the convenience store by way of the deserted lot that is infested with poisonous snakes and scorpions. I signed in, then wandered to the halfway house sidewalk facing Main Street. As I sat on the curb, sipping my soda in anticipation, I waited for the policemen to give the word. Finally, after several minutes of conversation, one of the cops explained the 'touch your finger to the tip of your nose with head up and eyes closed' game to the defensive driver. This guy played Simon Says with the cop and continued through the field test to walk the line. He then attempted to stand in place with one hoof off the ground, knee at chest level. More questioning from the officers ensued. I didn't stick around to see him get cuffed and stuffed.

That experience was important. As I watched the police officers make the guy squirm my past came back. I began to reflect on the good times, as I usually do when I start thinking about the old days, but I concluded the brief interlude by looking at the drunken state that landed me here. I used to battle with the past, but now that I can see clearly it doesn't take long for me to look through the good times and remember the drunken mistakes, which settles my mind and confirms that I have arrived at a better place.

I know what I'm doing now, and I like it that way. I feel good about myself and everything that I've done in the past several months. The rewards are staggering and I've begun to realize that there is no limit to my success if I remain sober. Without the drink, my life is calm, cool, collected. I don't need any more black out errors under my belt. I have the wisdom to know the difference today, I have the courage to change the things I can and I've learned to accept the things I can't do anything about. Today I live life on life's terms. This is a peaceful way to exist and I have grown to love it.

Day 78 Sunday, August 6

Today I got some letters out of the way and I received the package my parents sent which contains *The Satanic Verses*, a Salmon Rushdie book that caused a stir in the literary world. I started reading the book but I don't know if I should get into this here in Fahrenheit 451 land, where they don't want us to read books that are not about recovery. Reading fiction is a way to step into the minds and emotions of other characters and stories, a nice break from the heavy hammer of the halfway house, but this title might be too divisive if Bart's crew finds it in a room search.

Paul beat me at chess finally, which capped off my eight game winning streak on the chess board. After the game Paul and I rode our bikes to the pool for an afternoon of Arizona sun and processed water.

At the pool I learned a full gainer and took it up to the high dive with success. A full gainer is when you do a back flip after bouncing off the board facing forward, as opposed to having your back to the water and your toes on the edge of the diving board. I also did a double flip off the high dive today. Next weekend I will do a two-and-a-half. You just have to go up there and get it done like everything else in life.

Tammy and I gave each other back massages. Getting a back massage in the pool from a pretty young woman is heaven. Today was the first time I've been touched by a female in three months. She got into the back massage and eventually let me know that she was beginning to "defocus". I understood what she meant. Good thing I was underwater. That's the last girl I give a back massage to in Mesa. This is dangerous behavior in Bart's kingdom so lesson learned, innocent as the public pool back massage was.

I talked to Paul about how we can still 'party' without the intake of foreign substances. It could actually be okay with the right attitude. I'll look sharp and know what's going on while everyone gets drunk all around me back at college. I could be a designated driver every single night. What fun.

Day 79 Monday, August 7

I am back home after another hard day at the body shop. Today is Bart's thirteenth anniversary of sobriety. That's commendable. It's been thirteen years since he killed his best friend in a drunken, drug fueled fight and went to jail, a story he talks about all the time. I have trouble fathoming one year of sobriety. I bet it feels great to get that one year coin.

I'm beginning to realize the difference between projecting and planning. I used to project in desperation to avoid the present as my expectations of the future were idealistic and unrealistic. These days I'm thinking about the reality of things, and in my new humbled state I am setting goals that seem like reasonable plans.

I have thought about going back to school lately. I miss college life and friends. Here at the halfway house my views on college have turned from negative to positive. When I got into rehab I was under the false impression that everything about college was as twisted as my perspective. Now that I am thinking clearly I realize that I was the one with the problems, so I look forward to returning to my school. My old thoughts on academia were about coasting once I became bored with school years ago. I don't want to just get by anymore. I want to excel as a student and in life. Marginal grades won't satisfy me. I get strong marks when I apply myself so that's what I want to do now.

It's funny to think that once I got used to being stoned every day freshman year I didn't consider that partying. I was under the warped impression that partying applied to excessive nighttime drinking only. Now I see the absurdity of this perspective. When my drinking started to walk the line I began to minimize rather than glorify my self-destructive inclinations, down playing my abuse. After another blackout I would casually sum the evening up as though it had not been out of the ordinary.

Friends were concerned later in my prosperous drinking career. People told me they worried about me. Some of my fraternity brothers kept an eye on me and cut me off when I got too drunk last spring after my suspension. This rails against all those people out there who hate fraternities and try to shut them down, as the Greek system in small college towns makes lifelong friends and memories. A number of friends said that an angel must be watching over me. I shrugged off the voices of concern, satisfied that some people seemed to care. "I'll be O.K.", I would say.

What did I get out of my misadventures? A party animal reputation. That guy? He's a fish! He could drink me under the table! I became a drinking legend in my own mind for a minute.

Day 80 Tuesday, August 8

Every couple of weeks bullshit starts to grow like fungus at the halfway house, and that's when Bart takes out the scalpel. He screams, he kicks people to the curb, he scares the shit out of us, he helps us find our humility and he flushes all the crap away until it starts growing on the walls of this place again. I don't know or care about the gossip that flies around here, which got Bart going tonight. I just go to work early, I come home late to dinner and a meeting, then I go to bed and do it again the next day. I don't have time for the negative stuff that can stew and I want to stay away from Bart's wrath.

On Sunday, Ted came around to my unit and we

caught up for a couple of minutes. I am beyond the point where every time I see him I've got to tell him my problems so he can call me an asshole and set me straight. My progress is obvious so now I can shoot the shit with Ted about a ball game or a nice car he saw, or I can listen to one of his riveting stories. I guess once a recovering drunk clears his head he can start to feel normal again. I feel like a regular human being today and I like the feeling.

Ted has lived many lifetimes and he is much more interesting than I am. Today he told me about the body shop he used to have and some of the projects he worked on there. He talked in detail about how he was once commissioned to restore one of Hitler's old parade vehicles for a museum.

Day 81 Wednesday, August 9

I got back from work today and before showering I took a look at my reformed self in the mirror. Sure, I have a crew cut, a goatee and raccoon eyes from my sunglasses so I look like a comic book character, but I like what I see now. I remember all of those miserable mornings, still plastered, reeking of booze and basement mung, looking in the mirror at a mildly beer-bellied, bruise-covered, hopeless freshman slob. Today I'm slim, tan and healthy. Most importantly, I feel that crucial inner strength inside of me all day long. I've worked hard and everything is paying off. My body and mind are working together again. My perspective, my attitude and my appearance have been radically transformed. I stand sturdy and strong now. I've become proud of myself again. I have changed and will be a better man for it the rest of my life.

I won the weekly title of "Bart's Most Improved Fuck-Up" at the meeting tonight, and the reward was ten bucks. There was wild applause then laughter, I went to the podium, shook hands with Bart and waved the bill in victory as I danced back to my seat. After the meeting I picked up a candy bar, a pint of milk and a pro football preview magazine. Here I gloat on the couch with my creature comfort rewards for being the most improved fuck-up of the week, happy as a clam.

Day 82 Thursday, August 10

Work was easy but not great today. Clem was busy fixing his wife's Suburban while six children ran around the shop, playing with dangerous power tools. I fiddled for hours with a piece of shit, busted car window we are repairing. I like to repair things but this was a pain in the ass. Some thorns aren't big but they take a long time to pull out.

I got back from work in a shitty mood, frustrated because I was frustrated. Can frustration be something completely in and of itself? Anyway, I was relieved to get to the meeting tonight, which cleared my head after a long day and reminded me to appreciate what I have.

Bart introduced a new element to the meeting tonight, which I found interesting. He called Tammy to the front of the room and she took a solitary seat that faced the group. Then Bart asked for everyone to 'take her inventory', so people started to tee off on her. The exercise is designed to instill humility in the subject by way of beating the subject up, as if we don't beat ourselves up already. When Tammy returned to her seat, wiping tears out of her eyes with the left sleeve of her oversized white tee shirt (her right sleeve contains menthols), I volunteered to take the hot seat.

For the most part everyone said that I was working the program pretty well. Criticisms: isolation, defensiveness, superiority complex, overanalyzing. I wanted to hear from the rest of the halfway house and get it out of the way now that Bart will feature the hot seat weekly. It's strange to face a room filled with addicts and watch them hurl all their darts at you. You just have to sit there and take it.

So I have to stop isolating, although I prefer reading, writing, making art or playing chess outside of a friend's unit as opposed to 'engaging with the community' when I am not working all day. Engaging with the community means sitting in the kitchen area, smoking tons of cigarettes, playing cards, joking around, gossiping. I get along with everyone, but I have projects to chip away at after work. As soon as I turn my head I'll be flying back to New York, so I have to use my time constructively while I'm here.

Day 83 Friday, August 11

After work I called home and spoke briefly with Mom and Dad. For the first time in three months I talked to my youngest brother Christian, who is seven. Our short conversation was great. I miss my little buddy.

When I was drunk I didn't miss anything at all aside from the occasional party. My life became an endless series of all nighters. I'd wake up cocked and try to piece together the previous evening. My brain just about fell out of my head after a while. All I wanted was the next buzz, so sober time became more frustrating as my drinking increased to outrageous levels.

I don't remember much of my first semester. I let each day slide by and at night I showered, changed, and went out to destroy myself again. The only thing I looked forward to was walking into the party. To all my friends. I'd consume heavily and fast, black out and wake up to another day of bullshit, feeling wrecked, devastated, worthless. I was going nowhere but I didn't care because I wouldn't let myself see the truth of my pathetic existence. Drinking continued to punch me in the face at every turn. I attempted countless times to give these vices up or at least cut down. In the first several days of rehab, I claimed that during the second semester in the spring I had gained control of my self-destructive tendencies. What a pile of crap.

Today I feel strong, sharpened, smarter, more open-minded, and with a sense of direction. My spirits have changed drastically, I have begun to cultivate a healthy life and I want to nurture it. I never want to turn back.

Day 85 Sunday, August 13

Last night I went to the public pool with Dell, Bruce and half the population of Mesa. A huge screen was placed at the end of the pool. Everyone got into the water and they fired up the movie Jaws on the big screen.

This morning I repaired the gear box on my bicycle, which has been on the fritz lately. Man, I'm happy it's working again. Last night, on the way back from the pool, the gear box attachment got tangled up in the rear wheel at full speed and was bent to hell. I'm surprised I didn't fly off my bicycle. I had to take the under attachments off, hammer them into shape, bend back the spring and reassemble the kit. If I had heard someone say that a couple of months ago I would have responded, "What in the world is that guy talking about? Sure, whatever you've got to do." Clem and Ted have taught me the methodology of repair, which is universal to an extent. The bike is fixed because I have learned the process of fixing something and I applied my knowledge patiently to the problem.

I'm doing well. This coming Thursday I'll have sixty days at the halfway house, so I've been sober for almost ninety days now. I can't imagine going back to the chaos. This way of life is so satisfying. Living simply and humbly in reality today is definitely my preference. Sobriety will get me to the places I once could only dream of.

I'm learning to be a man these days. As Ted would say, "kiddy-shit" no longer works for me. Either I'm a prick about things or I continue to recover, and I'm not going to sacrifice my sobriety to be a prick again. I've been given the strength and courage to accept life on life's terms, and that's more than I ever could have imagined as a drunk. I'm living my life. Life is no longer dictating to me, and I like it this way. I don't need to search all over the place for serenity anymore because it's right here with me, wherever I go and whatever I do.

This is a simple whopper. There are complex moving parts to this way of feeling and seeing, the results of sustained hard work on my mind and body.

Day 86 Monday, August 14

During the first half of the meeting tonight Lenny explained in tears that he is in a great deal of pain. He fell down the stairs last night and has been sitting around all day with an excruciating backache. He's a big, quiet, proud man, so it was a shock to see him crying. Bart got Nathan to take Lenny to the hospital for x-rays. I think people were giving him shit today for not doing his chores and he finally couldn't handle the pain anymore. I hope he'll be okay. It is always weird to see a big, tough guy break down.

The meeting discussion drifted into the realm of tough family experiences. I talked about my home life and the problems that I encountered with my family when I got drunk. When I spoke with Dell after the meeting, as we sat outside on the halfway house bench smoking cigarettes, he pointed out my apparent detachment over the past month or so. Dell had some decent insight. I have spent the last month working an excellent program technically, but I seem to have drifted from the emotional side of things. He suggested that Bart takes such a hard, unbending approach that it's easy to go numb and play defense. Bart's philosophy is that we're the only ones to blame for our problems and it's as simple as that.

I've been living a life of compliance here in the trenches of a brutal program. "You're a no good asshole!" Yes, you're right Bart. This shit gets drilled into our heads all day long, and the rough edges that compose this halfway house bring out the survivor in me to make it through without getting booted. Bart says, "This is how it be," and I say, "Yup", because the slightest rebuttal sparks a torrential downpour of destructive, degrading criticism, not to mention the fact that it also endangers my position here as a 'hard working client'. I think, partly in response to the methods that Bart and his crew utilize, I have been forced to cast my emotions aside in order to endure. Dell slapped me with a flounder in the face tonight, which put me on my toes again.

Day 90 Friday, August 18

Clem is financially strapped this week so I worked with Ted for two days. It was odd not working a full week. Ted told me some great stories. He was a millionaire oil man twice but he lost both fortunes because he was a drunken, philandering 'asshole', as he put it. He often says that he can't believe his wife has stayed with him after all of his antics. He talked about growing up, getting in trouble, and going to jail for a short stint when he was eighteen for something minor. The old timers took a liking to him and taught him chess. He won an 18 and under state chess tournament by reading his moves over the phone from jail. He talked about how he once fused two trucks together. He cut the beds of each truck off and welded the front ends together so the vehicle had two engines with two ignitions. This allowed him to drive his new truck in either direction. He would pull into a parking space one way, get into the cab facing out with a different set of keys, and drive that side of the truck away so he never have to back up! Apparently this confused the hell out of people, who crashed their cars in amazement when he drove by. The state eventually requested that he take it off the road so he gave his double-headed truck to a museum. I would love to see that thing someday.

Thursday night I got my 60 day halfway house coin. Bart's chips are for however long we have been at his place. He doesn't trust where any of us came from and he calls rehab bullshit, not real sober time. I went to a meeting later in the evening outside of the halfway house in order to receive my 'outside' 90 day chip, as I have really been sober for 90 days. When I was a kid we all got trophies, but it's been awhile since I have earned a symbol of accomplishment like these little coins that mean something to me. As a member of my ambulance service in high school we got gold stars to pin to our EMS jackets when we brought a cardiac arrest patient back to life or when the crew performed well on a really bad call, which just came to mind and was a significant token of achievement in my recent past. Gold stars for the EMS jacket and varsity pins for the high school jacket.

Last night the staff told me to move to apartment #105, where I will be the new unit manager. My job is to keep the unit in order and report to my 'superiors'. Instead of having to stuff my few belongings in a small cubbyhole, I get the closet to spread my things out in. My deodorant goes on this shelf, my boxers go here, the pictures of my little brother go there, the photo of Sarah goes here, my books go there. The unit manager gets to enjoy an army locker as opposed to a small hole in the wall.

Day 91 Saturday, August 19

My bike has been giving me trouble lately. I've got to untangle the wreckage and take a peek at all the damage. I only have a couple of bucks to spare now, and I hope that I will be able to cover the cost of the repair parts. I finished my ninth book this week. I want sixteen books in as many weeks.

The weather has been normal, hot and dry, 105 degrees to 115 degrees during the day. Dry heat is an oven but it feels clean, easier in some ways than the humidity of the Northeast in July and August, when everything drips. Lately there has been wind, and the clouds after sunset are getting heavier.

I spoke with Mom and Dad last night and they sound peaceful. Dad pulled my old BMW out of the shed and it started up nicely. This is the first time he's mentioned my BMW since I drove it into the driveway senior spring. Now that his oldest son is getting his act together and working in a body shop my father has taken an interest because it's something I care about. I thanked him for checking out my car, by which I meant, "Thank you for paying attention to something I care about Dad."

Matt went to wrestling camp with his co-captain last week and he just got back yesterday. At camp Matt won a take-down tournament, which shows his potential. Wrestling is the sport for Matt. If he keeps it up he could win the States next year. He's earned his co-captain position on the team.

I got a letter from Walter, who sent me some music. I haven't heard my music in three months so I sat there in ecstasy while I listened for an hour and made a drawing.

I feel strong and serene these days. I know what peace of mind is today. There is no going back. My life is coming together fluidly, more than I ever could have asked for. I didn't know such freedom and happiness existed.

Day 92 Sunday, August 20

This morning I spent several hours with Dell. Lately we've been good listeners for one another. I talked about my strong support system at home and school. I have a lot of good friends so I won't get any crap about being sober as long as I am firm about it and leave my friends alone with their own habits. I will be my only obstacle.

It's an odd feeling to return home while all of my friends will be back at school, but I think it will be good for me. I can spend most of the fall mending ties with my family, working hard and going to meetings. I wrote to Sarah and told her not to make a big deal of my situation when she gets back to school. I told her that I look forward to seeing her on a weekend visit in the fall.

My bicycle still needs fixing. Hopefully I can take care of some of the mangled back wheel later in the afternoon. I have to bend metal and take things apart, which I don't look forward to, but I need my bike, my my transportation, my lifeline to freedom.

I've got a feeling that Ted will be spending more or all of his time in Clem's shop over the next few weeks. Clem has a complete overload and his business is strained. Ted only part times it here at the halfway house so he has hours to help his old friend. Since Clem is trying to finish some of these cars to get paid, and Ted will be there helping him, I don't think I'll be a necessity at the shop anymore. Clem has been getting sidetracked with tangent projects that don't bring in the bacon lately. He has six kids, his business is slow and he doesn't seem to know where to go with it right now. Maybe I'll haggle for some part-time work and get a couple days a week for my last four weeks here. Who knows? I care about the shop but work has been choppy and Clem's hard luck emanates out of the place. I need work days but nothing is solid there now.

My two boxes of belongings at school are at the fraternity in the storage room, and I wouldn't mind having Ben keep an eye on my stuff so it doesn't get torn to pieces before I get back. I tried to get Ben on the phone but I reached his mother instead. When his Mom answered, I almost hung up, but I stuck with it. I let her know that I hoped Ben would look after my things, and he could use whatever he wanted. I suggested that Ben put away anything he wouldn't use so it wouldn't get trashed. I told his mother that I'm doing well in Arizona, I plan to go back to school in January, and I look forward to seeing her son and the rest of our friends.

Day 93 Monday August 21

My apartment mate Ed is a new gem. He's a nice guy, but this three hundred pound man is a real pig, comparable to my old roommate Lonny from rehab. Ed is slow as a slug and walks around like the Hunchback of Notre Dame, with this giant gut of his, a stoop, his body crooked from overindulgence, gravity wearing him down. Last week I pleaded with him to take his socks off in the bathroom next to the air duct. He makes these grotesque, inhuman sounds all day long, and his snoring wakes me up at night. I've had enough of his filthy habits but I'd be an idiot to request another apartment change. Bart would tell me to fuck off, he would put me on restriction, then have his staff members move my bed into Ed's room and position it at his feet. I'll grin and bear it.

Day 94 Tuesday August 22

I just spoke with Matt for half an hour and it was good to catch up with him. He filled me in more about wrestling camp as he prepares for his senior year in high school. I admire my brother's lifestyle. He's taken the more mature path as a young man than I ever did. Instead of party-seeking or self-inflicting damage, Matt tends to take things as they come. He'd rather enjoy a relaxing weekend evening with several friends and a couple of drinks than a wild weekend bender. He seems to savor the important moments in life, and he realizes that these times are not eternal. I gobbled precious moments seeking instant gratification. Instead of working hard in order to enjoy and relax, I would work hard then spend my free time running my mind and body into the ground.

Now I am amused at the ignorance I displayed last year. I cared only for extremes and found pleasure in making the mouths gape on people around me. My methods of achieving attention were blunt and effective. The heads turned and I would get the commentary, good and bad. However much I got wasted, the excitement level in my life never exceeded a dull roar. After a while it all boiled down to the same old thing. Nights became predictable and monotonous. The only thing that was left to cheer me up was a case of beer. Yeah, that's original.

At college I'd snooze my alarm for the fifteenth time, I would open my clouded, bloodshot eyes from a blackout sleep and stare vacantly at the crack in the ceiling above my futon. My head would be swimming and I would have no clue as to who or what I really was in those waking hours. One of my morning rituals was to spend a minute clearing my throat into the padded garbage can as I was smoking weed and cigarettes heavily. I'm sure my neighbors didn't enjoy that too much. I guess the drunk has just woken up, because here he goes again coughing up lung butter. And it's only noon. It's an easy day for our next door neighbor today. After clearing my throat, I'd sit up and lean against the scalding radiator to smoke the morning cigarette, the one I always put behind my chair every night before I went out because I was such a planner. I would smoke there in bed, trying to recall what had happened the night before. What did I do last night? Who was I with? How did I get this abrasion on my arm? What have I missed already today? What day is it?

I'd stagger to my feet, turn the music on, limp down

the hall of the dorm toward the bathroom, a very respectable sight, agonizing over every step, hair down to my shoulders, cheesed over, farting and burping, coughing up brown phlegm chunks the size of marbles, half-erect from the aching bladder I had to relieve, the works.

I'd shower up, clean my room to hide this dismal state from myself and others, then smoke weed. On those occasions when I'd crack a book or go to classes I'd do it to pass a course with the 2.0-and-go strategy. After dinner I'd shower, dress and repeat the party procedure.

Days faded into weeks, and weeks faded into months like one of those cheap pharmacy paperbacks. Time meant little to me except for the magical mask of my 21st birthday, which would legalize my abuse (still two years away from me here in Mesa). As living in the present was depressing I remember all the brooding and false projections. "What have I done with my stinking life! Next year things will be much better," I would lie to myself.

Day 97 Friday, August 25

This week has been really good. Ted has picked me up in the mornings because he has been helping Clem so work has gone by fast. These days I take my time and have pride in what I do at the shop. I don't watch the clock like I used to. I think that knowledge instills pride and takes the monotony out of various kinds of work. Now, when I look at a current task at hand, I think about the bigger picture of making a car beautiful as opposed to sanding a door, for instance. Auto restoration is something of an art form, and I'm beginning to enjoy it.

Ted left the halfway house this week. His philosophy clashes with Bart's, and after a heated exchange on Monday he told Bart that he would be moving on. These recovery gurus are strong-minded individuals with opposing styles, and since Bart owns this place Ted was the one to go.

If anything, Ted's departure has strengthened our friendship. I still see him, there's no Bart rule against that, and our time together is more significant now that he is less accessible. Every time I'm with him is special these days as he is always dispensing pearls of wisdom into my brain. I just shut up and listen. He has taught me so much about life and about myself.

After work today I treated Ted to coffee. We sat at one of his favorite diners for an hour and he told me about a lot of things he's done in his eventful life. I can listen to his stories as long as he wants to talk.

I had a really good conversation with Mom and Dad tonight. I don't know why, but I always feel compelled to tell them about the progress that I've made. I wonder if that goes beyond the point of sharing and gets into my old pattern of people pleasing, which I have to stay away from. In any case I enjoy sharing with my fully supportive parents because right now they mean so much to me.

Right now I'm kicking back to a beautiful Friday evening sunset. Clem is having a tough month, so I won't work more than a day or two next week. Mom and Dad are paying the last week of rent so that leaves me a week to come up with. If I make any more than that I will get some paper for my journal.

Dad is booking a flight for me on the 17th of September. My spirits could not be better. I just have to do my best to stay in the present until it's time for me to leave Arizona.

Peaceful, happy, and free are crucial words of my existence today. I have come so far, and I can feel the progress now. I am much stronger than I ever would have been as a drunk, and I have become a young man with direction. I couldn't ask for anything more.

Day 98 Saturday, August 26

I signed out of the halfway house and rode my bike to the 7pm movie with Paul and Bruce. I don't know if the movie was worth it though because we missed the regular evening meeting. When we got back to the halfway house Bart screamed at us for ten minutes because none of us had been to a meeting during the day. The veterans here can go to outside meetings if they want to but the general understanding is that halfway house residents have to go to a meeting every day. Bart tore into us, he told us how fucked up we were and that we were riding a thin line with him. Bart got me back on my toes I guess.

Day 100 Monday, August 28

People, places and things have been topics that I've avoided. The conventional wisdom is that a recovering person can never go back to his or her old people, places, or things because they all trigger relapses. I am the only one who has changed so I have to realize and accept this. I can't get out of here and suddenly rejoin my old buddies in the places where I used to get wasted. I can't afford to take serious risks by rushing out there to test my boundaries at this early stage in my recovery, when so much is still new to me. I have to learn my limits and that will take time.

Day 107 Monday, September 4

Last week was hectic but worthwhile. I got a temporary job with Pepsi as a stock boy for the Labor Day blow out bonanza at one of the monster grocery stores in town. Pepsi had this big sale and people went nuts. The prices were so good that people were frantic and I thought there might be a stampede. My hours were 11am to 10pm and I worked my ass off. I started on Friday and worked Saturday until this crate runner nailed me in the ankle with his cart. My ankle swelled up like a melon but I kept working on it. The manager made me quit after looking at the bloody, gnawing injury and exclaiming, "Holy Shit!" at 5pm. I tried to hang in there but he insisted I get off the floor and rest it for a day. It was no big deal except that I had to lay off of it Sunday so I missed a day of money making. I was back today for the last day of the sale. Mountains of soda cases sat on palettes in the storage area and my job was to haul cases of soda out to the display area. People took them so fast that we were practically running to keep the display area stocked. The job was mundane and exhausting. Work is better than no work, although a lot of bums around here would disagree, so I am not complaining and I was glad to get the temporary job. I'll be able to pick up my check on Friday and that will cover my balance with Bart until I'm out of here.

Clem told me last week that he would call me but he never got around to it. I just want my last check and I will be on my way. Clem means well and I am grateful for the experience that shop gave me. I had a job for a spell, I learned body work and I can take my newfound knowledge to the old BMW that has been sitting dormant in the shed at home for a year and a summer.

Sarah's letter came the other day. She's doing well

and school is rolling along. It was nice to hear from her and I look forward to seeing her one weekend after I get settled back at home.

Home. Wow. The halfway house has been my home for so long. For the first time I can remember, I appreciate my family home I left in May, the family home I will return to in twelve days. I have done well by staying in the present recently. I have resisted the brooding of past and future, and I have grown stronger at shutting those thought patterns down when they come up. Everything has begun to come together as I grow healthy, and I like it this way. I'm on 'short time' now.

Day 108 Tuesday, September 5

Yesterday Mark the string bean blitzed the rooms and 'seized' four bags of books, two bags of books being mine. He really has a thing against books. I wonder if he can read. He communicates like a caveman so I'm not sure. He found the books I have already read in a kitchenette drawer, including *Satanic Verses*. There were three unread books that I hid behind a broken panel in the closet that Mark thankfully did not find.

Mark did the room check when I was at the mall getting another backup inner tube for my bicycle. When I returned before dinner, Bart and his wife were on the way out the door, heading to their big black Caddie. Bart was obviously pissed off, and when he saw me pulling in he motioned me over in anger. "What the fuck you been doing up in there? You been reading about Satan, you motherfucker? I ought to throw you out on your ass right now, you twisted asshole!"

Bart's not the kind of guy who would accept such a logical response as, "But Bart, that book was a literary firestorm in the publishing industry and this is why I picked it up." If I had defended myself like that, Bart would have called me a fucked up intellectual midget (one of his very favorite terms) and he might have tossed me out or put me on restriction... for a book. So I apologized to Bart, I said that it was not a cult book but a fiction book that someone had recommended at school. He tore into me, I took his verbal abuse and serious warning that I had better watch my step and stick with the AA material only or he'd kick me to the curb, even if I was on short time.

Shit. Any book with a title like that is viewed with suspicion. No, Bart, I don't light candles, cast spells and dance out there in the desert with my big bad cult book. What a hectic nightmare that was.

My Pepsi job ended last night. I spent my final shift making six-packs out of odd cans and cleaning up a massive spill for hours. 200 cases had toppled over before I checked in. I am proud to say that I helped clean up and mop the disaster area. What an honor. I was working with a couple of marginal guys who spoke matter of factly about their lots in life. "I'll work until my back gives out, then I'll pick up workman's comp and start teaching grade school. Damn! All you gotta do is make sure the little shits don't fall asleep on ya, right Al?" The thought of stacking products in a warehouse for decades was tough so I stayed busy and away from their depressing dialogue.

I started getting an attitude, thinking I was better than this stocking routine. Experiences like the Pepsi job have helped me realize that I should live life to the best of my abilities with hard work and passion. That doesn't mean I can get all cocky and think that I'm better than a job or some other person because I'm not, and neither is anybody else for that matter.

Day 109 Wednesday, September 6

Today I received a letter from my jailer rehab buddy Pat. It was good to hear from him. Pat, Randy and I spent a lot of time joking around and talking about everything when we were in rehab. Pat told me that Randy got out and picked up again. The more I think about it, the less I am surprised. Randy always spent his time helping other people when we weren't laughing our asses off together. Randy went to visit Pat and asked for a loan because he had to make a 'car payment'. Come on, Randy. An addict knows when one of his own is full of shit. Pat gave him the money and off Randy went.

Randy and others have fallen back into the merry-go-round, the downward spiral. They will be forgotten by the few of us who stay clean, so I will try to learn from these examples. I have found a unique group of individuals who help me strive, who scold me or lend a hand when I need it as I build upon my new foundation, my new life.

I am full of gratitude and peace these days. I work hard, I enjoy the down time to read, write and make art, I look healthy, I feel strong. What else could I ask for?

Day 110 Thursday, September 7

Yesterday I finished my fourteenth book of the summer. I spent the afternoon at the town park yesterday with Dell. On Thursdays there is a Narcotics Anonymous meeting in the park, and it was nice to go to a meeting outside for once.

Today I gave Matt a call. He is doing a college tour with Dad for a week, and they leave for the South tomorrow. I told Matt to take the trip seriously and get the most out of it because I did not appreciate my time with Dad like I should have when we had looked at schools together.

Now that I mull over those words of wisdom I shed on my brother I have to laugh at myself. I should be talking. I remember when Dad dragged me all over the East Coast and down South on two or three college tours during the fall of my senior year. Trying to get me to look at schools was like trying to get a dog to take a bath. We stayed with distant relatives and friends who could not have been more welcoming, we dined with old, friendly, tipsy professors who had taught my father when he was in college. They all had their pieces of advice. "So, you are looking at colleges, young man." If I had received a quarter for everyone who confused my decision making I would have made a hundred bucks.

I hated the school tour thing and settled on a decent college after spending a ridiculous weekend visiting the campus with a friend from my hometown who went there. As I waited for the next plane, because I'd missed my scheduled Sunday morning flight, I remember thinking about the weekend I had just had. I thought to myself, "The weekend was a complete blur, there are pretty women at this school, I got a nickname in one weekend, my parents will be pissed as hell that I missed my flight, so this is definitely the school for me!" I had in fact gotten a nickname in one night. There had been a massive, rainy Pig Roast party. I brought some LSD from a recent run of concerts, I smoked a ton, drank a million beers and partied all night with the guys who put the gig on until the morning, I rolled down the muddy hill, I laughed by the fire, and I amused the party throwers so much that they called me 'The Prospective'. When I got to school freshman fall people would walk by and say, "Hey... remember the Pig Roast? There is The Prospective!"

I remember the relief when I received my first acceptance letter, which came from SLU. I had just gotten my first DWI and home was a living hell, so my parents had some good news to temper their anger and disappointment in me. My father could no longer tell me that I would never get into college. No more college decisions. No more pressure, or so I thought.

Dell has finally decided to return to the East Coast and try Vermont. He thought about joining the Armed Forces for awhile, mostly because he wants to please his disciplinarian father. His new revelation is that it's okay not to hide from the fact that he has a secure financial life. For a long time Dell thought that by going into the military he could douse his past life of luxury and make something of himself from scratch. He told me today that he doesn't have to do that anymore. Running from who we are and where we come from is unnecessary. Dell and I have both learned that here at the halfway house. He said he feels inner peace because he has come to a resolution. When people stop beating themselves up, which drunks and addicts are really good at doing, they feel better. Facing the past is difficult, but it has to be done and it is an important key to recovery. If I can remember my mistakes without beating myself up, the new history I am making highlights the progress and peace of mind I have today.

Day 111 Friday, September 8

I just finished my book here at the old town library, a recent refuge outside of the halfway house, a peaceful place to read, to write and to think. I also don't have to worry about being thrown on the stake and torched for reading non-AA material, which gets tedious. I am close to accomplishing my reading goal. I'm getting into mystery novels. Old, burned out detectives sift through human behavior and emotions to solve their cases. I've gotten pretty good at analyzing my old state of mind so I find it stimulating to get into the heads of characters now that mine is untwisting. Novels are a painless way to do that.

Iraine wrote and told me that she's already sick of school. She is getting off of one of those soul-searching wilderness program summers. She's back on campus with a heightened awareness and she's pissed at the college kid syndrome around her. I empathize, but after a desert walkabout of my own I look forward to returning to college. I miss the good humor and laughter with my friends, among other things. When I get back to school I think they will support my new ways. And if someone gives me shit for being the sober boy? I won't get caught on the barbwire of some loser's drunken tongue, and I can always ignore negative commentary as well if it comes up.

I received a letter from Sarah today on a piece of ripped notebook paper that said in big letters, "Everybody misses you!" That makes me feel good. It has a nice sound to it, and I hope that ring stays in the air. Being missed, or missing anyone, was not something I ever really thought about before this summer, aside from the dead people I love and miss and would like to see again who have left my life.

Day 112 Saturday, September 9

These days I'm drawn to writing. The journal has been very good to me this summer. Sometimes I opt for the journal in pensive moments because writing is often more appealing than the endless loop of recovery language around here, and journals don't talk back.

I paid Bart's wife Pam the last week of room and board. I am certain now that the term 'board' here means the two by four holding up the ceiling in my kitchen. My unit is a piece of crap, the ceiling is caving in, but I am not complaining.

Dell will be leaving the same day around the same time, so we will go to the airport together. I'll have someone to shoot the shit with while we wait for our planes. Dell and I have been on the same tour schedule since the first week of rehab. He has become a good friend and I will miss him.

I have built a foundation and my growth has been big. I've come to realize that it's time to live in the present and to live life well. I don't have to put things off anymore because I have the time and energy to work on goals every day again. It's funny how much time I have now that I am not wrapped up in the party. Some recovering addicts wonder what to do with all of their free time but I have no problem diving into projects like I always have. I have redeveloped realistic goals. Work and dedication create success and achievement, which satisfy, nurture and inspire. These are all important things I could never manage when I was drunk.

I no longer have to worry about what people think of me because my behavior and actions are once again based on honesty and trust. I had no hope as a drunk and I have done something drastic about it. Nobody is going to take my hard fought ground away from me. Nothing is worth the price I have already paid to see clearly.

I've been sober sixteen Saturdays in a row. I'm on a roll because I know in my heart that I have learned true strength, and I can move on from here with continued success. I was ripped out of there just in time and I've made the most of it.

Day 113 Sunday September 10

Today's adventure was excellent. Andy is a second month resident and the only one with a car. Andy, Dell and I hopped in Andy's restored BMW and headed for the lake, which is one of the things that halfway house people try to do while they are here. The drive was amazing. The feeling of freedom and a light heart overcame me as we cruised down the strip, heading off towards the range of mountains. The sun beat down and the wind flowed through the car, refreshing and warm. The music blared and I got tangled up in tunes as the desert drifted by on the endless road.

The beach was one of small pebbles. Clean water. Big lake. I haven't seen a natural body of water since the day before rehab, when I drove to the beach and cried on the rocks in all of my anguish and self-pity.

The lake was nice and the water was great. I took several dips, just enough to get cool. We spent the afternoon lined up on the beach, with our white, Bart-issued towels which barely reached from our heads to our tailbones. I cracked my new book and started to feel the mounting plot anticipation that means I will race through the book. It was a perfect day.

I couldn't get my mind off of restoring my BMW

when I was riding around in Andy's car today. He happens to have an orange 1972 BMW 2002, which is some coincidence. I can see my BMW now; jet black, polished trim and hub caps, custom license, sparkling BMW emblems, perfect interior, loaded. Every day of work, every hour, every minute in the shop this summer I have dreamed about fixing my car up again.

Day 114 Monday, September 11

This is my last Monday in Arizona. I called Clem, and in his usual monotone voice he let me know that there was no work this week but I could pick up my check. I have $13 plus what Clem owes me, which should amount to almost $50. I'll try to find a buyer for my bicycle as I would be overjoyed to leave on Sunday with a hundred bucks in my pocket. When I get home I'd like to avoid asking my parents for a buck here and there until I find work.

I rode out to the body shop for old time's sake. The ride was long and clean as I reflected on a summer of change. I walked into one of the open garage doors and it was good to see Ted again, who has been at the shop to help through Clem's rough patch. Ted showed me the carefully engineered hinges he made from scratch to fit the hood of an old Packard he was working on. He showed me the latch he built that will be mounted and wired through the interior compartment to a knob for the driver. As usual, Ted had designed and created this elaborate system, which was better than the hood system on the original car off the assembly line. I gave him his due credit as he showed me the slop just under the rear wheel wells. "Uggh!", I told Ted. Inches of crusty bonding coated the rusty metal, which indicates a rip off job by another body shop before Clem and Ted got their hands on it. Then Ted showed me the fender work he'd done on the car. He had clipped the rusted metal and had welded on some perfectly sculpted replacement parts that he had fashioned from scraps. It was inspiring to look over a car with Ted. He approaches his work like an artist. I asked if he was free this week and he told me to call at 5pm.

Before I left with my final payment in hand, Clem showed me the finished Mercedes that I had worked on this summer. The Merc was buffed to its original navy blue with fresh, polished chrome. The old car is gorgeous once again. I am grateful to have had the chance to learn that auto restoration is an art form. My mind drifted to the BMW several thousand miles away and I wondered for a moment what sandpaper to finish with before painting my BMW. I answered my own question - 320, then wet sand with 400 like always.

I shook hands with Clem, I told Ted I'd give him a call, I said goodbye to the shop and I peddled away. I will gladly remember all the good times at Brand's Reconstruction and Repair. The experience I gained there is something I will always have under my belt. I'll send before and after photographs of my BMW to Clem and Ted and I'll make them proud to have taken a chance on me.

I got back from the library this afternoon and went over to Ted's trailer house after calling to make sure he was home at the end of the day. Dad was good enough to shoot a video of my car and send it to me. I hadn't seen the video so it was something that Ted and I could sink our teeth into while chain-smoking and drinking coffee.

To begin with, I have to replace the rocker panels, fenders and quarter panels. Although it will cost me more to replace everything, Ted said that it will eliminate any fruitless attempts for me to save certain parts from the grave.

In the seals, around the trunk, I've got to grind, cut out and patch the rusting areas directly under the protruding rear shocks. In the engine compartment, I have to grind and patch the cracking, rusted areas in the front corners of the support frame. Ted told me that the 1971 BMW 2002 is a unibody, as opposed to the less sturdy, mantled pieces that comprise many car frames these days.

When I return home I can start my long term project by cleaning the crap out of my car, taking off the fenders and rockers and going to work on all of the rust. I can also take off the trim and polish it up nicely. Ted suggested that if the trim is stainless steel I can hammer some of the dented and bent trim pieces into shape, but Ted has the feeling that the trim is plated.

I don't have the time or money to spend on my car all at once. In order to work towards all the goals I have created for myself, Ted said that I should spend a little time on the car after work every day and it will start to shape up.

We talked while Ted chipped away at the 1500 piece jigsaw puzzle he started this week. That puzzle is impressive. We spoke of Bart's place, and Ted joked a little bit about the ways of the Mesa Halfstep. We discussed the dynamics of hard work, setting and adhering to goals. We talked about Ted's idea of doing restoration at Clem's shop on the side.

Ted told me to treat my car like a child, to mend it and take care of it. He said that it looks like what I look like, and as I get stronger the car will become beautiful again. He said that restoring this car would be great, that the rewards would be tremendous. He mentioned that a restored 1971 BMW will be some prize in twenty years, and that I ought to hang onto it when I'm finished. "You'll be lucky to have that fucker in a decade or two," Ted said, with a cigarette dangling out of his mouth and a couple puzzle pieces in each hand. The time went by quickly, and I told Ted I'd give him a call later in the week.

Our meeting was at 7pm as usual. Bart eventually rose, took to his podium and started going on like he always does at the beginning of each meeting. "You fucking addicts" this and "you fucking addicts" that, he yelled. Then, there was a glimmer in his eye and that shit eating grin appeared on his face as he waved his cane around, cracking the dais or a nearby table for effect. Everyone sighed in unison, under the impression that he was in good spirits tonight. But just as people were beginning to relax he pointed at Red, a young guy who had been in my rehab also, and screamed, "Now Red, you get your skinny ass off my fuckin' chair, take your flea-bitten shit, and get the fuck off my property right now before I shoot you with that gun in my big motherfucking Caddie out there! Nathan, go unlock Red's door and get him the fuck off my property now." From what little I heard, Red had abandoned his roommate in town to meet a young lady he'd met earlier in the week, which is taboo. Bart's explosion was harsher than usual and scared the shit out of everyone. I wish Red good luck, that poor bastard.

During the meeting I volunteered for the hot seat again, and this time I got more than I bargained for. "You are self-centered, isolating, resting on your laurels, planning results, angry like a bird in a cage, defensive, lacking spirituality, lacking humility, a perfectionist with an inadequacy complex." The community hurled spears at my ass one by one with enthusiasm. It never gets old to face thirty people who raise their hands, look you square in the eye and throw this shit at you, whether or not their editorial is accurate. You can't say anything. Thank you sir may I please have another.

Bart summed everyone's comments up by saying that I had potential but I was a stupid "motherfucker" resting on my laurels. I'm glad I volunteered for the hot seat tonight. I got some slaps in the face to wake my ass up. I wanted to hear Bart's angry voice, and I sensed concern in what he had to say, as if this was his way of wishing me good luck. He knows I've learned what I needed to learn out here, but he wants me to 'keep it green' and he doesn't want to see me mess my priorities up. It was a goodbye Bart style.

I've matured into a young man here, and day by day I'll continue to forge ahead. I'm not in this place to please other addicts. I'm here for myself and no one else. I'll do it in spite of the people who think I will fail if that's what it takes. I want to be able to call Bart with a year of sobriety and say, "Kiss my fucking ass because I made a year." Bart enjoys getting this phone call from people who reach a year, something he repeats in his meetings all the time with laughter.

Day 115 Tuesday, September 12

Last night my father filled me in on his journey South to visit colleges with Matt. Mom and I had a peaceful chat. She has made me feel very good the last few times we have talked. She says they just want to love and support me when I return. I look forward to going back home and settling down again but I'm scared to death so Mom's support is very much appreciated.

This summer has been the best experience of my

life. Aside from pulling my head out of my ass, I've logged five hundred pages in journal entries, I have read a book a week, I have worked on my sketchbook steadily, I have learned about car restoration, I have made some amazing friends, I have turned my life around, I have learned to like myself again, and I am out of here in four days.

Day 116 Wednesday, September 13

I saw a dollar movie at the mall today. There was a character in the film who was an artist. I didn't like the art but it was cool to see an artist's studio. I would like to spend my life making art for a living. Who knows? Maybe some day that will be a possibility.

I started getting down in the dumps before the meeting tonight, rationalizing for a moment that I might have some party time left in me. One minute I'm on top of the world and no one can touch me, but then, when I least expect it, that monkey climbs up on my back again out of nowhere and starts whispering in my ear, "Come on, man, just have one." This is the hardest thing to deal with, and in order to stay sober I have to defeat these spells of weakness. They say it just gets better, those old hands who have been sober for years. I've been away four months but suddenly I'm in the trenches again when these feelings come on. I guess with time and dedication those bouts will become smaller and less frequent as they have for me in the first 120 Days.

Temptation kicked my ass for awhile today, but a good meeting and some Ted talk got me out of it quickly. I called Ted after the meeting and asked him about weakness. He smoked while he talked, "Either live the right way, working hard and enjoying reality, or spend the rest of your life fucked up. It's as simple as that. We addicts are fucked up people. It's all or nothing to us, and that's the way it goes. It's not easy, but you'll keep learning if you work at it. I have faith in you, son. Hey, at least now you have come to accept that you're one fucked up cookie, like the rest of us, and you've found people who understand." I thanked Ted and said goodbye. That man has taught me a world of things, and sometimes I wish that I could have a couple of chips off of Ted to keep in my wallet. When in need take two Teds and call in the morning.

Day 117 Thursday, September 14

My unit mate Ed left tonight. He's had enough of Bart and the halfway house, from what he told me. He misses his wife and kids and he thinks that he has learned the tools he needs to stay sober, like so many of the other people who give up and leave early. I wish him the best of luck. On a lighter note, I won't have to experience any more of his grotesque personal habits. No more Ed farts, bowel movements, foot odor or snoring for the last several days of my stay here.

Dell and I have talked extensively about what we're in for when we return home. I still have a lot to prove to myself and to my family, but it will be much better than living here and I am cautiously optimistic. Trust will come faster because I've already pulled off four months. They say that second-timers have a much harder time getting sober and regaining trust. I want my family and the thought of losing them scares the hell out of me. I don't want to have to go back to the first day again. I know what I have to do now to grow.

Today I received a letter from Wayne, one of my best friends from school. Wayne says that school is the same as usual. He has a decent room that is well situated on campus. He enjoyed a lazy bum of a summer, living at some girl's place until her parents got back from their house in Bermuda. He kicked around from house to house, waterskiing and windsurfing, partying, dating the pretty college girls. He even did a little house painting to support this difficult lifestyle. Wayne is right when he imagines in his letter that I've had a more productive summer. I'm not the one who's saying, "Gee, I wish it was the first day of summer again." I've got my pom-poms out and I'm doing back fucking handsprings in my falling down apartment. I'd fly home on the landing gear of the next puddle jumper if they'd let me.

I no longer envy my friends for their fun summers as envy has faded from my radar. I did what I needed to do for myself this summer and I have no regrets today. This is miraculous but actually true.

I've been thinking about the future as usual. I can never keep that out of my mind. Get back home, work, write that children's book, make art, go back to school. I always try to map out my whole life. You cannot possibly do that in one sitting, you numbskull! I guess I want everything now. I just have to put one foot in front of the other as I am on the right path at a healthy young age. "And you know what, all you fucked up addicts? I know all this because I be eating steak every fucking day!" Bart screams from his podium throne while he wipes the corners of his broad smile with a handkerchief and laughter boils in the audience.

Day 118 Friday, September 15

I beat Paul in our farewell chess match. Paul got sick of this place, like so many other people, and left before dinner this evening. I wished him good luck and watched old Pops drive him away.

Bart called a makeshift meeting this afternoon. "Some of you is gonna help me or I'll be damned. Now empty your pockets, come on, three dollars from each of you. Don't be cheating me on your nice banquet, you cheap motherfuckers." Dell and I will be receiving our 90 day chips and graduation papers tonight. Bart splurges for a Polaroid shot of him shaking hands with his graduates. Maybe I'll take that Polaroid, blow up Bart's face and make a dart board out of it.

9:30 pm Journal Update

I wanted to shower before I received my certificate so I had to wait while my other apartment mates took showers. During that time Bart awarded Dell with his graduation certificate and made fun of me. When I got down to the meeting room at 7:10pm I asked for my certificate and photo. Bart told me to fuck off because I had "shot my wad" by being ten minutes late. I wanted that picture of me shaking hands with Bart, and now I'll never have it. I guess it's not my problem and I should let it go. Bart has his own tough style and I'm out of his world in two days. I didn't realize that Bart would be handing out our graduation papers promptly at 7pm. There were only two of us anyway. 88 days invested in this fucking halfway house. I shouldn't dwell on it. I don't have to prove anything to anyone but myself anymore. Bart can be a prick and that's not my mantle to carry.

I called Ted several times but he wasn't in. I guess I'll try him tomorrow. I'm really psyched about getting home but I wouldn't mind a cup of coffee with Ted before I leave Arizona. I will miss Ted a lot. I will not miss Bart.

Clean, healthy, refreshed, alive, electric, happy, peaceful, free, energetic, optimistic... this is how I feel as a four-month-old and I love it.

Day 119 Saturday, September 16

Four months. It's hard to believe I'd ever come this far and it feels great. I'm a lucky young man.

Dale drove a group of us to go tubing today. The sun was blazing, the water was refreshing, and there were pretty girls who floated in our vicinity during the four hour river glide. I haven't been tubing like this so today was perfectly Arizona. I let my mind drift with the flow of the currents. It was nice to spend Saturday away from the halfway house.

When I got back I finished packing and went to talk to Bart. After several words he covered up for his nasty streak last night and Pam grabbed a graduation sheet for Bart to sign. He shook hands with me and Pam clapped so my private graduation ceremony was complete. Before they left for the night I hugged Pam and said I'll keep in touch. They were good to me overall. Bart's actions are his deal and I don't have to hang on to the unnecessary behavior of others anymore.

I chaired my last meeting here and the topic was gratitude. It was a good meeting and at the end some fellow addicts wished us luck.

Seth asked if I would join in the evening apartment unit discussion after I got organized. I sauntered out with my cigarettes, blinded by the ugly light, and took a seat facing the couch. The nightly ritual began and the four of us talked about what we are doing here, how our days go, what runs through our minds here, what is on the other side of this place. I shook hands with my apartment mates and hit the sack.

I travel early tomorrow. I leave the books to be found by someone else behind the closet panel. I take with me a backpack of belongings, my journal, my hard work, my humility, and my peace of mind.

Day 120 Sunday, September 17

Dell came in and woke me up. "It's 5am... time to go." After I showered and packed the remainder of my belongings I walked out to the halfway house ferry. Dell and I threw our bags into the back of the orange meat wagon. We turned to the halfway house at dawn, we looked at each other and smiled, then we got in the car. We were off in a flash of Mesa morning, long strips of road, the sun bubbling and the hair on my arm standing at end with the windows down as we barrelled towards the airport.

We parked, I got out with Dell and we pulled our things out of the 'limo'. Pops got out slowly, dressed in his standard panama shirt and black polyester slacks. While he shook our hands he said, "Have faith and you can remain sober day by day." We walked in through the roundabout doors. Pops peeled away with cigarette smoke streaming out the driver's side window, off to resume his life, a man I would never see again like everyone else that I loved and hated, laughed with and cried with, lived with and worked with this summer.

We checked in and talked feverishly while smoking

butts as the coffee set in. When it was time to part ways we hugged, shook hands and I watched Dell fade into the migrating crowd.

Dell means a lot to me. We've come through this four month journey together all the way. He has been an inspiration and we've shared so much together. I wish him the best in life.

I remember many times in Mesa when my thoughts of returning home were sparked by the overhead distant drone of aircraft. When I saw a plane fly away into the sun out in the desert I would think that one day I would leave Arizona behind and feel the joy of complete accomplishment. I have done very well for myself this summer and the day has come to leave this place. I will continue to grow stronger at this promising young age in life. The halfway house has proven to change everything about me in a positive way. I have graduated from Bart's place and will leave it, but this place, this city, this state will always be a fond memory. Here's to the state of Arizona and it's good people.

I never did get a hold of Ted. I tried him a bunch of times yesterday but he wasn't in. He will hear from me soon enough. That man showed me the way to live happily, peacefully, and freely. His work has done wonders. He has taught me so much about life, the program and about becoming a man. For these things I will remain eternally grateful. I respect his placid and soft spoken nature when he's not calling me a fuckin' asshole. He has shown me how simple my world can be. We are the ones who complicate the whole thing, so we have to stay out of the way and let go. He has shown me that I cannot control people, places or things, so I just have to remain content, do the footwork, and let life flow by softly. Words cannot express how I feel at this moment as I wait to board my plane for New York.

We stopped in Dallas Fort Worth for ninety minutes so people deplaned. I ate a slice of pizza and read about these mysterious crop pattern swirls in Southern England farm fields. When I boarded the plane again someone had taken my newspaper, so I got on with my new book. We landed on time in the late afternoon, a topic that had been discussed often at the halfway house. Suddenly I was back East. Wow.

When I arrived in New York I exited the plane with butterflies in my stomach. I drifted slowly up the gate ramp with the rhythm of the crowd, taking in my new surroundings as I was swept along by my fellow passengers.

I made my way down the baggage claim stairs and saw a grouping of my family's feet, their legs, their bodies. I saw my mother's pink short sleeve shirt, her nervous arms crossed, then I saw their faces, my mother's tears, her joyful expression. I walked to my mother and embraced her, then my father and brothers surrounded us and I felt the warm glow of family.

I was home.

 Sandy Garnett, *Mesa Mandala*, ink on paper, drawn in Mesa.

Back home with the old BMW

4

The Closer

(Half A Life Later)

© SandyGarnett.com, working on Twister paintings in his CT studio

I returned to live at home, I worked locally, and I went to a meeting a day until I returned to college for the spring semester of sophomore year. My friends were supportive. I took my newfound energy and threw this into a fine art career. I had business cards printed and chased bands around, making art for musical acts while I was in college, doing their CD covers, backstage passes, posters, logos, tee shirts and mailers. I lived in my fraternity until we all got thrown out, I poured beers behind the bar at parties sometimes, as I could see the action and I liked the energy around the bar, but I remained sober through the rest of college and beyond.

People may be under the impression that I was tempted to start drinking again at college, but this was really not the case. I was so humbled by the Mesa Halfstep that all I wanted to do was walk a straight line and prove any doubters wrong when I got out of there. I applied this stubbornness to my art career, which became the vessel for all of my energies in college. Art is strong because it will absorb any energy you throw at it.

The hardest thing about returning to school initially was that I didn't want my friends to feel awkward around me if they were partying. This just took a little time, but it quickly helped me to feel normal with my peers again. Once they realized that I was not passing judgment or uncomfortable they forgot all about the fact that I was sober. I eventually became a confidant for every drunk on campus who was thinking about cleaning up his act. The key thing was to be a good listener and never get on a soap box. The second hardest thing was learning how to date without the social lubricant of alcohol, which flowed all around me and often into my dates as well. Normal people figure this out, so I learned like everyone else.

My freshman year I missed class and didn't do the work so my grades sucked. When I returned to school I became a good student again. I learned how to enjoy school, I was aware of how free and lucky I was to be there and I used this time to build my new fine art business when I was not in class. I started to work very hard at whatever I did in college, remembering and employing the work ethic I had left behind at the end of high school, the work ethic my parents taught me that has stuck with me through life.

I wanted to graduate with my class so I took extra credits to make up for my missed semester. Senior year I was granted an independent project to edit my 500 page handwritten journal from Mesa into a 300 page working manuscript. My professor was good enough to read and help me edit the first two drafts.

The summer after graduation the late Nancy Murray of Fifi Oscard Agency in New York City had editors read my manuscript, both of whom said it would publish well. They asked me to do another edit and then bring the manuscript back to them, which was exciting news. A week later my computer crashed and my book was entirely deleted along with every computer file I had ever made to that point in my life. My backup was a second computer, and since they were linked together and crashed together both drives were lost at once. Tough luck, lesson learned.

I took this blow in stride, life moved on and I built a fine art studio that I have been running since graduation from college.

Several years ago I dug up the only surviving hard copy of the first draft and started chipping away at it again. I had done a lot of writing since this first manuscript and I had more books in me, so if I was going to publish a first book it would have to be this one.

Everyone knows a friend or relative who has lost his bearings. Often times people never come back. In my case I sorted myself out, I grew up, and I used my experience as a platform to build a rewarding life and career. This is a story that would have helped me had I read it way back when, day by day, so it should be useful for those who are going through recovery, those who are trying to find direction, and for people around them who care.

I maintain that this was the best experience that ever happened to me, the pivotal moment in my life. I was given the opportunity to peer inside myself, peel back the layers and make some fundamental changes that have made me who I am today. It wasn't easy but it worked like it can work for other people who have the determination to make personal changes. I learned in Mesa that I can't change others but I can change myself if I put the time in. Without this experience I would not be making art for a living and of course this *Baloney* book would not exist.

I never did get around to fixing the BMW. I had a landscaping company with my friend Dave the summer after Mesa and we made good college money. I took the entire summer's earnings and bought two quarter panels, two rocker panels and a fender (read: not a good use of summer college money). I had a shop weld the rocker panels on but they did not cut the rust out underneath the rockers as they said they would. The car sat and I returned to school. I started making art for bands in college and this interest superseded auto restoration clearly, as I drove a pile of crap Plymouth Reliant K car, the ultimate girl magnet, for five years. My Dad was always a point A to point

B guy, not a car guy, and I followed suit, the apple falling very close to the tree. "Do you see me with toys?" my father asked. "The answer is no. I don't care about the toys." My mother agreed. "That's what I like about him, he could care less about the toys." There the BMW sat in the falling down shed for many years until I sold her online for five hundred bucks to a father and son racing team who came down from Massachussetts to pick up their new piece of crap. The father drove Porches and the son drove a BMW 2002. They loaded her up on their trailer while talking about their weekend racing, their auto shop, the 27 BMW 2002's they have lined up in a lot for spare parts. They got a good deal, I unloaded a shit box, and my parents don't have that old clunker in their world any longer, although it was fodder for endless family humor. Maybe I should have kept it for the comedic prop that it had become.

Last night my parents called and asked if I'd like to join them for dinner. We sat at one of the family places, a down home steak house where we have gone to celebrate the highs and get a reprieve from the lows in family life over the years. I was wondering if this was family business, but my parents were in good humor, back from a small trip, so our dialogue meandered lightly until another family came in with a little hellion in the pack of six who stood on his chair and started screaming. I couldn't focus on our conversation as the kid took over the room. Parenting came into the scattering dialogue as tables around us adjusted to the distraction. Nature versus nurture. I had dated a woman and had helped raise her son while we'd been together in my early twenties. I get along with kids and I had been a good stepfather for those several years. "You never know with kids. Sometimes they are just very hard and sometimes you wonder if the parents let them get away with murder. You can't say anything," my mother noted. In this case the child was clearly going bananas and his poor parents had to remove him from the table. My father chimed in, "No, you can't say anything. Like our friends who have two bratty grandchildren say, you just have to zip it."

Dad asked about the book. I told him it was coming along, that I was enjoying the editing process while I worked on the book design and painted the cover illustration. I talked about how good it felt when I touched back down in New York to my waiting family on day 120, how surreal that day had been for me after a summer in Mesa at the age of 19.

My mother turned and said, "I was scared to death. You know, I've never told you this before, but I remember that day when we went to the airport like it was yesterday. We all stood there nervously and then I saw your feet, your legs. I was terrified. You were walking down the stairs towards us. I saw your shorts, your shirt, then I saw your eyes, I saw YOU, and I said to myself, "There he is. There is my son. I have my son back."

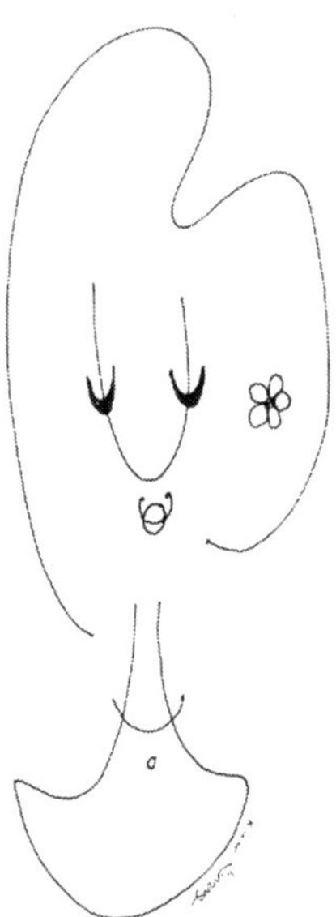

© Sandy Garnett, *Garnett Girl*, MMX.

ACKNOWLEDGEMENTS

It was a real kick in the cookie to have a manuscript after graduation that seemed on its way to publication, only to lose the entire computer file I had spent six months working on. Going back to square one required some serious energy, so my early readers were very important sounding boards who helped me bring *Baloney* into the light after many years.

I would like to thank Deborah Shea, who edited the first draft with me in college, for her belief in my writing and for her support of this manuscript.

My galley readers were Annie Edgerton, Claire and Steve Garnett, Christopher Peter, Brooke Garnett, Bill Edgerton, Matthew Garnett, Kim Harris, Alex Garnett, Kristina Young, Christian Garnett, Phillip Dolcetti, Jennifer Klopp, and two friends who read early drafts while they were in rehab, both of whom strongly recommended *Baloney*. As I did not have the support of a traditional publishing house, I threw every aspect of *Baloney* at my team. Each reader assisted in the editorial process. Special thanks goes to Annie Edgerton for notes on several successive early drafts and to my father Alex Garnett for proofreading the book with me a number of times down the stretch. My early readers kept me motivated and focused as this book took shape over time in the background of my fine art career, so I am very grateful for their enthusiasm, their patience and their valuable insights.

I would like to thank the people that I went through my 120 days with way back when. My case manager was great, as were the therapists whose solid work helped to open my rebellious, sleeping, bloodshot eyes. This goes for the patients in rehab and residents at the halfway house that I made fast friends with. I would like to thank Dell in particular for being there every step of the way. I have to grudgingly thank Bart for smacking my head full of good sense and miraculously teaching me new swear words in the process. I also need to thank my parents and my brothers for being the best family a fine artist could ever ask for, then and now.

Most of all, I want to thank Ted, whose positive influence at a pivotal moment in my life changed me forever. I'm afraid this book does not do justice to the dynamic range this mentor brought to my table, equal parts hard ass and good old cowboy, but his backbone and his willingness to snap me back into shape ring loud and clear. Although I only spoke with him once or twice after I left Mesa, Ted is alive and well in my heart if you haven't already noticed, and he will always walk alongside me through life. As I write these very words I can hear him ask between cigarette drags, "Why didn't you fix up that BMW like I showed you how, you peckerhead? Come on then, let's get some coffee, on me."

It's good to get this monkey off my back that grew into an 800 pound gorilla over twenty years. Onward and upward, as a friend of mine likes to say.

Respectfully,

Sandy Garnett

Garnett with his Installation of 312 Fingerprint Portraits
at The Aldrich Contemporary Art Museum, Ridgefield, CT, 2010.

ABOUT THE AUTHOR

Sandy Garnett was born at Fort Belvoir, Virginia and raised in Pennsylvania, London and Connecticut. He is a self-taught fine artist and has made his living as a painter and sculptor since he graduated from St. Lawrence University. He lives and works in two studios he bought and renovated in Connecticut, and he works in New York City sporadically.

Garnett signed his 1000th career painting during the first publication of this book.

www.sandygarnett.com

In The Works

ADVANCE MENTIONS

"A MUST READ."
- Alan Abel, America's Most Famous Hoaxer

"People need to laugh these days. I think this book will be enjoyed for it's self-effacing, observational family humor. This book should be called 'Tales to Feed Your Schadenfreude'."

- Christopher Peter
Astute Cultural Critic

"First of all, I love the cover. It's hysterical."

- Annie Edgerton
Broadway Actress

In The Works

ADVANCE MENTIONS

"This book should be mandatory reading for art schools."

- Dennis Bradbury
Gallerist & Curator

"Every artist will have this book because of the title alone. This is a riot."

- Lina Morielli
Fine Artist

"A book about how you survived as a professional artist for 20 years? I'll take the first copy."

- Fellow Artist